AN ILLUSTRATED HUMANIST HANDBOOK FOR OLDER PEOPLE

Compiled by
Dr Alan Burnett

AN ILLUSTRATED,
HUMANIST HANDBOOK
FOR OLDER PEOPLE
Alan Burnett

Design © 131 Design Ltd
www.131design.org
Text © Alan Burnett

All rights reserved. No part of this publication may be reproduced, stored in any retrieval system or transmitted in any form or by any means, electronic, mechanical, photocopying, recording or otherwise, without the prior written permission of the copyright holder for which application should be addressed in the first instance to the publishers. The views expressed herein are those of the author and do not necessarily reflect the opinion or policy of Tricorn Books or the employing organisation, unless specifically stated. No liability shall be attached to the author, the copyright holder or the publishers for loss or damage of any nature suffered as a result of the reliance on the reproduction of any of the contents of this publication or any errors or omissions in the contents.

ISBN 978-1-909660-32-8

British Library Cataloguing in Publication Data. A catalogue record for this book is available from the British Library.

Published 2016 by Tricorn Books,
131 High Street, Old Portsmouth,
PO1 2HW

www.tricornbooks.co.uk

TRICORN
BOOKS

AN ILLUSTRATED HUMANIST HANDBOOK FOR OLDER PEOPLE

CONTENTS

Foreword from Jim Al-Khalili 7

Acknowledgements 10

Introduction 11

1. Humanism for older people 15
2. Sunday Blues. *Some personal experiences of religion, the church, science and humanism* 19
3. A quiver of quotes, quick-witted comments, and quips:
   a) Ageing and Old Age 25
   b) Religion 36
   c) End of Life: Death, Dying and Afterlife 66
   d) Non belief, Atheism, Agnosticism, Scepticism, Free Thought, Science and Secularism 77
4. Hurrah for humanism 96
5. Stats and Maps 109
6. Secular Giants. *Robert Ingersoll's life and views on making the best of later life* 117
7. The Peppered Moth. *Let's hear it for Charles Darwin, and tell our grandchildren about evolution and explain diversity in the world* 126
8. Special objects, people, places and events; clever (church) conversions. 137
9. Let's be Positive. What humanism can do for us, and we can do for humanism.
   a) Leading a good life without religion. 143
   b) Striving for a secular future, or at least an even playing field 145
   c) Let's be positively humanist 148
10. Good books and rich resources 150

Permissions 155

FOREWORD *from Jim Al-Khalili*

A criticism I have never really understood that is often levelled by some of those of religious faith against the secular is that somehow, by arguing that there is no higher purpose to life, and nothing awaiting us that will prolong our existence once we have shuffled off this mortal coil, our lives are therefore bleak, meaningless and humourless.

For me, and just about every secular humanist I know – and I know quite a few – this is a quite ridiculous notion. Once we acknowledge that this is our single and short at life, that seems to pass us by, gathering pace as we get older, then we are even more likely to cherish and celebrate it than those who may be holding out for something better in an afterlife. Therefore, approaching life and all its trials and difficulties with humour, as Alan Burnett does in this delightful book, seems utterly natural to me.

Although mine and Alan's paths had crossed now and again over the years, the Venn diagram of our lives shows that we have overlapped, mainly through family connections, in various unexpected ways. Yes, we are both university academics, though in different institutions, and we are both committed atheists and humanists, but that doesn't tell you the half of it. Alan was a Portsmouth City Councillor some years along with my father in law, which was when I think I first met him; he and his wife Jenny have for many years been close friends of my parents in Southsea; one of his daughters was, and still is, a close friend of my sister's and another daughter dated my nephew when they were teenagers. This cannot be accounted for by some 'small town' argument – Portsmouth, where we both still live, has a population of over two hundred thousand.

Most recently, our paths have crossed at meetings of the British Humanist Association (BHA). Alan first told me about this book at the World Humanist Congress in Oxford in 2014 during my tenure as president of the BHA and I promised him I would write this foreword. The BHA, like other secular humanist organisations around the world, works to correct injustices and unfairness in society whenever and wherever certain groups are given privileges or advantage because of their faith, or where those without a religious faith are treated unfairly or discriminated against. For example, an ongoing campaign is the BHA's work on fair admissions in schools and to put an end to religious selection in state-funded religious schools that discriminate and indoctrinate, but to have instead an open and inclusive education system that will educate children together and not segregate society. Other campaigns include important human rights issues, such as support for assisted dying. It all sounds like a serious business – and it is. But, I should stress that humanism is also about celebrating life and what is positive about the human condition. Humanist celebrants for example conduct hundreds of weddings, and thousands of funerals in England and Wales through the BHA's provision of meaningful non-religious ceremonies. A million people a year in the UK attend a humanist ceremony – funeral, wedding or naming.

Of course, secular humanism, as a way of life, is not itself a religion; it is not a cult or a movement, nor does it have some insidious agenda to spread atheism or talk people out of a personal faith that is important to them. To think that is to pander to the silliest of conspiracy theories. It is also true that not all humanists are atheists and nor are all atheists humanists. Indeed, while one may define atheism as an ideology, it is also not a religion. I have heard it said that atheism is no more a religion than not collecting stamps is a hobby, or the off button on your TV set is another channel.

I came to discover that I was a humanist not because I was 'converted' – I was a humanist long before I knew that I was. I simply came to realize that those human traits and attributes I hold dear, such as empathy, tolerance and kindness are what define me as a humanist. But it's more than that: it's about having faith not in the supernatural, but in humankind's capacity, by and large, to be decent. I thought I would become more cynical as I settled into middle age – but I'm pleased to report that my optimism and hope have grown stronger over the years.

Many might find it sometimes hard to maintain optimism and humour in an often humourless world. We have seen in recent years a rise among certain corners of society of an ugly intolerance, whether it be religious extremism or bigotry and discrimination towards minorities. We are not all of us brave enough to rise up and fight the many injustices in society, so do we instead hide away, sulk and complain? Well sometimes, yes. I mean who doesn't? But, you see this book provided an important and welcome antidote. Alan Burnett shows that humanism is something to celebrate and enjoy.

Do I believe the world would be a better place without religion? Well, in a utopian sense I suppose, yes, it would be nice to live in a world in which nobody feels the need to believe in a supernatural omnipotent creator to make sense of the world and their place in it. But this isn't going to happen any time soon – and a reasonable argument can be made that the world would be a pretty boring place if we all thought and believed the same things.

We all of us know, I'm sure, many people with a deeply and genuinely held religious faith who do not feel inclined to impose their beliefs on others, or to be given special privileges in law because of it – these are decent people who do not deserve the derision we might pour on them for holding what we might regard as silly views. After all, we must acknowledge that, for millions around the world, faith provides comfort, social cohesion, a sense of identity, belonging and hope. All these are undeniably important traits. This life-affirming book, written and compiled with a humour and light-hearted honesty, shows how secular humanists hold all these traits too. That having a rational view of the universe and our place in it and celebrating our all-too-brief stay on this earth are all also cause for hope, celebration and joy.

Jim Al-Khalili
October 2016

ACKNOWLEDGEMENTS

Jenny and my wonderful family Tom and Lisa, Otis and Rosa; Kate and Matt, Keir, Elsie and Edith; Helen and Trevor, Etta, Jesse and Asa.

The late professors John Milburn and Jim Riordan; officers and members of Portsmouth Pensioners' Association - past and present - and my former colleagues at Help the Aged.

Also Howell Jones, the Al-Khalili family, Mike Barrie, Joy Foscett and my sister Didy, and late brother David. John and Janet Quinn, Ron Sonnet, Tom and Roses Graham, Anton Jansz, Elizabeth Hughes, Marianne and Fröde Vangsne, and Sonia Vidal. Claudia Bradshaw, and many more in Portsmouth, elsewhere in the UK and the rest of Europe, USA, Ethiopia and the world

Special thanks are due to Gail Baird and Dan Bernard of Tricorn Books, as well as Lee and Laura Asher of AsherDesignandPrint, for their professional input and personal encouragement. Their expertise and help has ensured that this handbook is both coherent, and superbly illustrated. Raphelina Bonito (*RMB*) and Trevor Toghill (*TT*) for the cartoons.

All the authors from whom I have learnt so much and who are quoted in this volume notably Greg Epstein, Marcus Brigstocke, Susan Jacoby, Philip Kitcher, Jen Hancock, Paul Kurtz, Bryan Niblett, Russell Blackford and Udo Schüklenk, Peter Cave, Peter Coleman and Peter Wilkinson, AC Grayling, Christopher Hitchens, Steve Jones, Louise Antony, Jerry Coyne, David Voas, Bruce Grant, Lois Lee, Bryan Tully, Penelope Lively.

INTRODUCTION

As you can surmise it has taken me several years to compile this handbook. I have enjoyed the process of discovering, digesting and distilling the work of others. I have learnt a lot, tried to create a coherent, well illustrated and interesting publication. I now want to share the fruits of my labours with others.

Of course I have been highly selective in my choice of material to present. The material included appealed to me and reflected my own outlook. It has provided me with insights into religion, non-belief and humanism. Much of it was chosen for its entertainment value (some readers may find its levity irritating). Nearly all of it is from books and journals written in the English language. So I readily take the credit and blame for its unusual format and the scope of its contents.

Professor Laura Carstensen, from Stanford University, has proposed a 'social-emotional selectivity' theory which suggests that in later life (with the end in sight) we tend to become more 'choosy' in our outlook and pre-occupations. And this seems to ring true in my own public and private life. I feel a strong desire to focus on good news, and be positive. I only like to watch sport when the side I support is winning. I cannot bear listening to right wing politicians or unctuous religious leaders. I recoil from ageism, racism or sexism when confronted by such prejudices.

On the other hand, I enjoy reading 'Private Eye for its exposure of the greedy, hypocritical, and dishonest country/world in which we live. I hate cruelty, injustice and exploitation wherever it occurs – on our doorstep, or the other side of the globe. I prefer to concentrate on the tolerant and liberal-minded features of our age. For me music and art, as well as family and friends, make life worth living. I love the science and beauty of television nature programmes; bird watching; and the changing seasons. But not seeing one creature killing another! I rejoice when I see or hear of 'small unseen acts of kindness and generosity'. I try to see the 'good' side of religion, while being horrified by violence perpetrated in its name.

I can readily understand why so many millions of non religious sceptics do not belong to humanist associations and secular societies. Most probably they have never heard of them or don't see the point. They just get on with their everyday lives. But for me, in my seventies, humanism with humour ticks all the boxes, and its time that we became more active in its cause, albeit in a tolerant and inclusive way.

Some devout people will accuse me of 'having a go' at religion. Some non-believers will question why, in a publication advocating secular humanism, I have spent so much time on religion. The answer is, as Richard Holloway so aptly puts it, because 'religion is still the biggest show on earth'.

Although religious belief and practice is in decline in many places, few would dispute that it remains a powerful force in the lives of millions of people round the world, not least amongst older people. But my case is that there is an alternative. That is non-belief in general, and humanism in particular.

It has been estimated that in a lifespan of 70 years in the West on average we spend 23 years asleep, 16 years working, eight years watching TV, six years eating and 0.7% of our life on 'religious' activities. (What about sex, sport and social media I hear you ask!) Producing this volume has certainly upped my 'religion score' in recent years!

My main assumptions in this endeavour are threefold. First, that religion is an integral part of most cultures. I learnt as an anthropology student in the shadow of Durham cathedral that religious institutions serve a number of functions – social, political and economic - in societies across the world. I happen to agree with Karen Armstrong that 'religious' conflicts often have wider cultural causes. Religion is not going to disappear anytime soon, but that doesn't mean that its power and influence cannot be challenged.

Secondly, that there is a growing global divergence between the general decline of faith (and rise of secular humanism) in the relatively tolerant West, and strength of religious fervour elsewhere. I have seen the latter at first hand in Ethiopia (where thankfully Christians and Moslems rub along together) and have also read about the horrific murders of non-believers in Bangladesh by religious fanatics.

Thirdly, there is evidence that both strong beliefs and humour are good for you, and that definitely includes us older people. Later life has its challenges. For many, BUT NOT ALL, religious identity and belief offers companionship and consolation. But for humanists there is no heaven, but the satisfaction of leading a full and useful life. If you google 'Humanism and Humour' you will find how laughing releases those lovely endorphins that make us feel better. You will also discover that the comedians Linda Smith was, and Shappi Khorsandi is currently, President of the British Humanist Association. If you delve further you will find that the agenda of many local humanist (Milton Keynes and South West London to name but two), and sceptics' groups contain light hearted debates. Dublin Sceptics meet in the 'Black Sheep' public house, and their official podcast is named – 'The Skeptrechauns'.

From the outset in my search for material for this publication I was seeking answers to questions such as - 'what do we know about the beliefs of older people and is it a matter of chronological age or cohort (the people living in a specific social landscape in time and place) that determines differences in world views? What elements of belief and disbelief – religion, atheism and humanism can help in later life? How can and do non- believers cope with the prospect of death? What motivates people of all ages to lead good lives? (Have a look at Greg Epstein's book) Although many church attendances continue to shrink in Western Europe at

Last, how come Humanism has not (except perhaps in Norway, where every year some 10,000 teenagers enjoy a secular 'confirmation' organised by the Norwegian Humanist Association – Human-Etisk Forbund) filled the void? Is it true that more people go fishing and visit car boot sales on Sunday morning in the UK than go to church? Why, as Richard Dawkins puts it, 'do humans fast, kneel, genuflect, self flagellate, nod manically towards a wall, crusade, indulge in costly practices that can consume life and in extreme cases, terminate it?' How and why are people of all ages in some areas of the UK, Europe, and North America more religious than others? What exactly is Humanism and how can it be put into practice in our daily lives? You may find some answers in the following pages.

Then there is the issue of what can be written to augment the rather dry and wordy books on these topics which are to be found in bookshops and libraries? How can humour be harnessed in the cause of humanism? Jokey books about senior citizens are readily available, but not very satisfying. There are illustrated and amusing collections compiled by clergymen such as Mark and J.John Stibbe – presumably used to liven up sunday morning sermons and spice up church magazines. Light hearted, irreverent books, with the notable exception of those like 'The God Collar' by Marcus Brigstocke, are few and far between. There are some very good books on old age and ageing to be read. My own favourite is Penelope Lively's 'Ammonites and Leaping Fish. A Life in Time'. Her sixty pages on old age are both perceptive and enjoyable. She is an agnostic who loves cathedrals, bibles and church music. Her chapters on memory and books make great reading. Her own 'treasured objects' (some of mine are also to be found towards the end of the handbook) are described with evident nostalgic fondness.

Searching bookshops and charity shops (I have found British Heart Foundation and Oxfam emporia are the best); ordering books and finding academic papers online has been exciting yet time consuming. My wife complains of the ever growing piles of books in the corner of our dining room. Classifying and grouping quotes and key passages was a tricky and tedious exercise (thank you Gail). As for the illustrations – photographs, maps and cartoons – they play an essential part in this publication. I hope you agree they enhance it.

So what is the scope of this 'humanist' handbook? What are the key components of its ten chapters? How have I arranged the wealth of material I have found into a coherent and readable volume? How much of the book is explicitly about my own personal experience, thoughts and actions?

I will answer some of these questions by outlining the contents and giving the flavour of what can be found successive chapters.

In chapter 1 you will find a justification of a project and why it is aimed at an older audience. Why it is full of humour; why I embarked on the project; why humanism, and other beliefs are good for older people (be they grandparents, patients, potential volunteers, or ordinary non-religious pensioners.)

Chapter 2 is largely autobiographical. It tells the story, decade by decade, of my own experiences and changing outlook. Others have written more eloquently of their growing 'up and out' of religious faith, but I hope that my background and changing outlook will strike a chord with some readers at least.

A quiver of quotes is reproduced in chapter 3 under four headings – ageing, religion, end of life and non-belief. These topics are in turn divided into over forty sub-sections in which focus on different aspects of the theme being presented. This is then followed by a similar organisational pattern when covering Humanism in chapter 4. In both these chapters a wide range of authors have been quoted. If there is any originality here it is that a sustained attempt has been made to bring some order and coherence to the table.

We all like statistics and maps and that is why in chapter 5 there are plenty to be found. Such a task is always contentious. Some statistics – local/regional/national/global will surprise and shock, and the maps are there to paint the spatial patterns of change and diversity. (By the way spatial memories are stored in that area of the brain called the hippocampus, and London taxi drivers who hold 'the Knowledge' have larger ones!)

If you are a sceptic or secular humanist you will be pleased to see that you are in good company in chapter 6. But most of this section of the handbook is devoted to the wonderful Robert Ingersoll – the 19th century American radical who is woefully neglected on the other side of the Atlantic. What an inspiration he was in his time and should remain so today.

And likewise there is Charles Darwin in chapter 7. So much has been written about this great English naturalist that there is hardly room for more coverage of his life, work and legacy. But far fewer people know about the peppered moth – a fine example of evolution in Britain over little more than a century. Other recent research is also cited which shows how modern genetics is explaining the processes whereby creatures, great and small, adapt to their environment over time. A good (true) story to tell your grandchildren.

Chapters 8 and 9 contain some more personal reflections and promptings. First, on how we non- believers can gain satisfaction and solace from possessions, people, places, past events – and seeing how religious buildings have been preserved and converted to secular functions.

Then what Humanism can do for us and how we free thinkers can further the Humanist movement. Whilst others may have set out a clearer and more persuasive path for action, please take heed of my suggestions for leading an ethical life, and campaigning for a more secular country and world.

In the final chapter a variety of books, articles, websites are to be found. Not exhaustive by any means, and in need of continuous update, but a good start to follow up and on from this handbook. If my selection of this wide ranging material leaves you wanting more then please go to the original sources.

This is a collection to dip into when you feel in the mood, and share with others. I hope you will find it both heartening and entertaining.

CHAPTER 1
HUMANISM FOR OLDER PEOPLE

A. Babyboomers

Like many other countries, Britain is an ageing society. It is high time that the needs, views and beliefs of the growing numbers and proportion of older people – in all their diversity – are given due consideration. While combating ageism, and campaigning for a better deal for older people – particularly those who are isolated, poor or abused – is definitely a must, so too is ensuring that their non material – some would use the term 'spiritual' – needs are addressed. In particular the growing minority of older people in the UK and elsewhere, who do not believe in God must surely welcome a publication which hopefully they will find illuminating, heartening, amusing and useful. As Ludovic Kennedy wrote – 'the timing is auspicious and the social climate conducive to a favourable reception' among the 14 million people aged 60 and over in the UK, and the millions around the world.

B. Belief is best

For Peter Coleman and colleagues at Southampton University strong beliefs held by older people – be they humanist, atheist or religious – contribute to their wellbeing.

In the chapter on 'Coping without religious faith: ageing among British humanists', we are reminded that strongly held secular views and a humanist 'life stance' can be good for you.

Elizabeth MacKinley is also a fund of knowledge on how older people – religious and not, see the world. She provides some rich insights, especially amongst the 20% of the sample reporting that they had no religion at all.

The Victorians viewed the irreligious as – 'friendless, tortured souls, prone to suicide and deathbed repentance'. Clearly there are many older humanists in the UK and around the world who are anything but so – partly because of the beliefs they hold and positive attitude to later life!

C. Built-in bias

The findings of the 2011 Census showed that there are a growing number and proportion of British people who have no religion ('even' amongst older people).

Yet national institutions in this country are overwhelmingly (and outrageously) still religious and mostly Christian. Of course the British Humanist Association challenges the presence of bishops in the House of Lords, the establishment and funding of 'faith' schools and the religious bias of the BBC in the form of the broadcast of religious services and priests pontificating on 'thought for the day'. Yet the religious near – monopoly of power and influence remains, despite the changing demographics of non – belief in the supernatural, so there is a strong case to be made for the separation of state and church and a more even playing field (or open and accessible public square) created as between religion and secularism/humanism.

D. Books

There are excellent secular books to be found in the library of Conway Hall, Red Lion Square in London. As Greg Epstein has noted there is scant choice when it comes to finding any real choice in bookshops. Scan the shelves of any new or second hand bookshop, or indeed charity shop and you will be hard pressed to find even a single slim humanist alternative to the ever present religious volumes. There are bibles to be found in hotel bedrooms, and glossy 'celebrity' magazines in surgery waiting rooms. With the notable exception of the publications of the British Humanist Association and the National Secular Society and its sister organisations, worldwide there is a woeful imbalance in favour of the religious in the nation's reading material. Understandably it is to a younger and more sceptical audience that most non religious writers have focussed their attention. Efforts have been made to tell the story of evolution to school children, (see Michael Rosen and Ann More Young's recent slim volume and Alan Shaha's *Young Atheist's Handbook*) a humanist philosophy for students. Older people have been largely ignored in this respect. Brian Tully's *Raising the Human Spirit* is a notable exception. This excellent collection of poems, prose and song lyrics is aimed at people of all ages living in a diverse, secular society.

This booklet gives a clear message to Senior Citizens—there is a humanist alternative and it might be for you.

E. Burnett's birthright

On a personal note, and bearing in mind my upbringing in a Church of England family, I have been generally content to see myself as a 'christian humanist'. I certainly would not go out of my way to denigrate religious faith and observances, although some of them appear to me foolish, outdated and even harmful. The growth of religious extremism, and the reluctance to change on the part of the British establishment, has jerked me out of my tolerant complacency.

Having Jim Al-Khalili as President of the British Humanist Society was a bonus.

Jim's family live in Portsmouth. Unlike the 'new atheists', (notably Sam Harris, Richard Dawkins, Daniel Dennett and Christopher Hitchens) Jim, with his Moslem/Christian background, appears to take a more 'inclusive' stance in relation to the role of humanism and critique of religion in modern society.

So its time to 'come out' publicly as a humanist. As far as my neighbours are concerned in Southsea's St Thomas' ward (super output area 022D) the 2011 census, showed a third of the population declaring themselves as having 'No religion'. Amongst older people like myself, less than 10% were of a secular persuasion. So I have a fair way to go to declare my locality as a religious free zone! In fact St Jude's Church down the road appears to be pretty busy, at least its community hall (from whence they distribute coffee and compassion) is never empty!

Greg Epstein maintains that age should not be a barrier to telling the story of humanism, he states, 'There are so many older people out there with more experience, more knowledge'. This Harvard University chaplain highlights the humanist message on the basis of his work with students and the community in Boston. I am concerned with making a positive contribution to the lives of older people in Portsmouth, England, the United Kingdom, Europe, America and the world.

F. Banter ... respectful but sceptical

It was George Bernard Shaw who asked if humanists had a sense of humour. He lamented the lack of laughter in the Christian Church, and urged sceptics not to take themselves too seriously. What better way to review academic and popular publications on ageing and belief/disbelief than with humour. As Greg Epstein points out in his 'campus tour' – 'sometimes the most forceful way to respond to our conservative religious critics is with humour'. A similar argument has been made by Mark Steel in *The Guardian*, in which he argues that pure science will not convince, but sceptical wit is more likely to do so. My stance is respectful but sceptical and quizzical, rather than deferential, or hostile.

We need to remind ourselves that on both sides of the Atlantic there is a rich tradition of free thought and disbelief. How many people in America have heard of Robert Ingersoll and in England of Charles Bradlaugh? As Charles Rudd has noted in a recent volume of the Ethical Record, these two secular celebrities of their time invited comparison and deserve greater acclaim. Both men were non believers who used plenty of humour in their armoury.

Thus this project aims to provide a readable and well researched 'mainstream' publication for the millions of older people in the UK and elsewhere who are sceptical about religion, and may like to be informed, amused and encouraged by an alternative approach. I hope it will find its way into libraries, be seen in airports and on cruise liners, in community centres and rest homes, in the waiting rooms of surgeries and hospitals, read openly on benches and beaches.

Please disseminate these chapters far and wide, and to people of all ages, but especially to those of us who are enjoying or enduring later life.

Welcome to humanism

CHAPTER 2
SUNDAY BLUES. *Some personal experiences of religion, the church, science and humanism*

Many distinguished writers have provided an account of their changing personal beliefs and growing scepticism, and 'secular conversion' from religion to agnosticism/atheism, and humanism. For example:

Louise Antony's book contains explanations of how eminent American philosophers emerged from Christian and Jewish backgrounds to secularism. Some express great affection for their religious traditions, even though they can no longer embrace them. Others acknowledge losses that can be suffered when faith dissolves. Many argue that secular life can provide rewards as great and as rich as those claimed by the religious. Amongst the most notable are the testimonies of **Walter Sinnot-Armstrong** who writes:

> *My childhood was inundated with Christianity. It's not that my family was especially religious. They weren't. It was just that they grew up in Memphis. Like most southern US cities Memphis was overflowing with Christianity. There were more Christians in Memphis than water in the Mississippi River. Just as the Mississippi was hard to escape when it flooded, so Christianity was unavoidable in Memphis, especially around Christmas, Easter and Thanksgiving. Anyway, I didn't try to avoid it. I went along, like any good child would. I could see church spires all over town…religion surrounded me in the air I breathed. Despite my qualms, I was not ready to give up religion yet. I still liked the songs and the spectacle. I've always had a weakness for stain glass windows and bible stories. The people in church were friendly to me. If I had renounced or denounced religion in Memphis, my family would have been shocked. So I stayed silent.*

And from another background, **Joseph Levine** writes:

> *From very early on I was subject to the conflicting messages of traditional (East European) Jewish life and modern American culture……storm clouds of doubt were forming.…..I suppose it took a few more years before I realised I had lost all my religious beliefs and indeed classified myself as a secular atheist. It wasn't until I lived in Israel…I saw at first hand how Jews treated Arabs the way Jews were themselves were treated in Eastern Europe. Let's be clear what founding the Jewish State of Israel involved and continues to involve. We came to another people's land – admittedly after enduring centuries of oppression ourselves – kicked them out brutally, and treated those who remained as dirt. We continue to oppress Palestinians horribly, and shamelessly exploit our own history of oppression and guilt-trip of the rest of their world into letting us get away with it. This is how God's people act? Not any God I wanted to have anything to do with, (pp 18-27).*

There are striking accounts of turning to humanist/secular thought to be found in the chapters of *50 Voices of Disbelief – Why we are Atheists?* edited by **Russell Blackford** and **Udo Schüklenk**. (Some of these are noted in chapter 3 and 4).

Ludovic Kennedy tells us how he questioned his parental and educational religious influences. His upper middle class parents took Christianity 'as read'. They did their duty and lived their lives according to their beliefs and principles. For Kennedy confirmation at public school was more or less automatic – like joining the OTC. Disbelief grew, although the insidious and all pervading pressure of teachers, older school mates, relatives, friends of the family, newspapers, the radio and establishment figures all conspired to encourage the continued , albeit temporary, belief in God and Christianity. Humanism beckoned in adult and public life.

> *'During my teens, although I continued to sing in church choirs, it became evident to my family that I no longer believed in the Christian doctrines in which I had been brought up ... I grieved for her (my mother's) grief'. He also continues to appreciate church music – 'Neither did I see it as necessary to abandon the music I loved, simply because it was embedded in the rituals in which I know longer believed.*

In *Living with Darwin* **Philip Kitcher** raises the issue of the effect of loss of one's faith on the sensibilities of much loved 'religious' parents.

Likewise some perceptive and heartening accounts of how disbelief grew in **Greg Epstein**'s *Good without God* (2009); **Paul Kurtz**'s collection – *The Humanist Alternative* (1973); and **Joan Bakewell**'s *Belief* (2005).

Alan through the decades

Here – in a 'decade by decade' autobiographical diary a few of my changing experiences and beliefs are recorded. They will surely strike a chord – at least amongst readers brought up in a Church of England household in post war Britain and who have become 'cultural Christians', 'atheist Anglicans' or indeed 'non believers and humanists.

Alan at school

1940s

- Born and baptised into the Church of England. Ancestors included Archbishop Ridley – burnt at the stake in Oxford, 'Keziah', a Jewess of London and numerous Anglican clergymen and missionaries.

- Witnessing and 'accepting' the death of wild and domestic animals being killed on uncle's farm in the Scottish borders.

- Visiting elderly relatives – including Uncle Charles and wife (former housekeeper) who had been missionaries in China. Upon their return he bought a bungalow and he installed a three quarter size billiard table in a converted hen house in their back garden. He played there every afternoon with his cronies. They gave me a mint imperial and half a crown which made my 'duty' visit worthwhile.

- Being a choirboy in the church at Seascale, Cumbria, was OK as we got to see and smile at the choir girls across the aisle. However, to get us there on time the crafty vicar supplied only 11 cassocks for 12 choirboys – the one who arrived last in the vestry had to wear an old raincoat instead! If we made a noise in getting to the cupboard where the clothing was stored the vicar would shout sharply – 'Shush boys, remember whose house this is'.

- The vicar of Scotby preached that it was harder for a rich man to get to heaven than for a camel to go through the eye of a needle. I used to wonder what the wealthiest family in the village who owned a business in Carlisle – sitting in the pew behind – was thinking. The only resident of this suburban village who owned a Jaguar car was a bookie, but he didn't go to church.

1950s

- Embarrassing moments: when the collection plate came round and I found that I had forgotten to bring a shilling – or spent it on Saturday sweets in the village shop.

- Despite growing scepticism, I went along with the confirmation ceremony – with the approval of my peers and parents.

School Report - 'a slow start in divinity'

- Met and was greatly impressed by Father Trevor Huddlestone. Wondering if I had the 'protestant work ethic', following a charge of being lazy in more than one school report.

Kudat, Borneo

- Whilst doing VSO, seeing missionaries at work in North Borneo – now Sabah – and having grave doubts about the value of what they were doing. Climbed to the summit of Mount Kinabalu (13,000 feet) and watching our local guide kill a chicken as a sacrifice to the gods. He subsequently, and very sensibly, cooked and ate the scrawny bird.

1960s

- Being mightily impressed by the architecture of Durham Cathedral when shown around during Freshers' week at the University of Durham.

- Read Evans-Pritchard's 'Nuer Religion' as part of anthropology course.

- Hearing from a college friend that in Manchester you were either a 'proddy dog' (protestant) or a 'mackerel snapper.' (Catholic)

- The vicar who married Jenny and I had grey socks and a reputation for poaching salmon from the River Eden.

- Painted a humanist logo mural in our back garden. It remained there for many years.

Anthropology student

- Witnessing a student in the Geography Department at Indiana University, whose assignment I had marked, fall to his knees in prayer to thank God for getting a good grade.

- Watching African American babies being born in St James' Infirmary in New Orleans and wondering what sort of lives they would lead.

1970s

- Experiencing at first hand the 'suppression' of much of religious activities in Ceausescu's Communist Romania. Christmas was not celebrated, but cards were sent, presents exchanged and bottles of excellent Murfatlar wine were drunk at New Year instead.

- Whilst on holiday in the Western highlands of Scotland drew frosty stares from 'wee frees' on their way to the kirk on a June Sunday morning. The object of their disapproval was Jenny giving me a 'home' haircut on the bothy front door step.

1980s

- Finding and purchasing (for 2/6) a battered copy of 'Selections from Ingersoll : A slayer of Superstitions and Slavery, Orator, Reformer, Rationalist, Humanist' in a second hand bookshop in Portsmouth. The previous owner was 'Hyland of 2 Kingston Crescent, North End, Portsmouth.

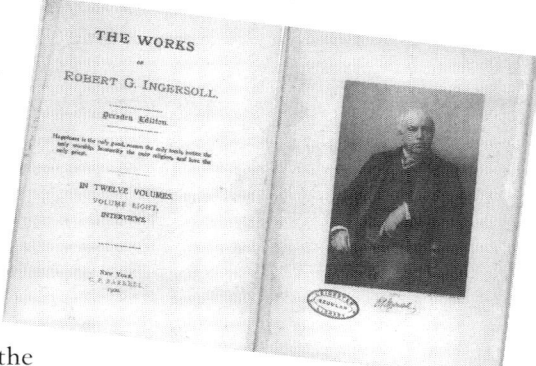

- Being asked by a female vicar who was conducting the funeral service for a friend…'Are you of the church'? Was Mrs X – the deceased 'of the church'?

- Hearing a woman in a bookshop in Swanage, Dorset asking for a copy of the 'God Delusion' by Richard Dawkins. She was informed politely that it was not in stock!

Best 2/6d I've ever spent

1990s

- Losing our passports in the Graham's house in Washington DC. They were only discovered after their Panamanian maid said a prayer to St. Theresa, 'the saint of lost causes'. She believed in the 'miracle' – we were mightily relieved.

- Visited Drogheda and was shown the remains/ relics of Oliver Plunkett in St Peter's church. A gruesome experience!

- Having grace said before every meal in our friends' house in Portsmouth, Virginia.

- Visiting several churches, a mosque, a Sikh temple and synagogue whilst Lord Mayor of Portsmouth.

2010s

- Walking out from a funeral service in the Portsmouth dockyard chapel in response to a traditional religious service and the unbearably unctuous delivery of the chaplain.

- Telling a joke about nuns to a party of Ramblers in Crete – to mixed reaction.

- Whilst staying with friends in Provence, we noticed in the local cemetery that Catholics had been 'laid to rest' in one half of the holy ground and Hugenots in the other.

2010s

- Nearly getting accidentally 'run down' by Richard Dawkins on his bike in Broad Street, Oxford after visiting the Natural History Museum and paying homage to Charles Darwin

- Deciding on a new goal for later life…' Keep fit, stay active and enjoy precious moments'

- Being visited by a hospital chaplain a few hours after having a hip replacement in QA Hospital. Politely declining his 'services'. Would have preferred to have a cup of tea from a pretty army nurse!

- Abiding memories of belief in Ethiopia, the country where Haile Selassie had become a cult figure to Rastafarians in the early 20th century. When asked how white cottoned worshippers outside churches managed to 'receive the word', our driver Melesse told us 'that angels came out to visit the faithful'. Mr Seyoum on the other hand – much to the incredulity of young men sharing a pizza – calmly announced that he was a 'free thinker'. For many years he had worked for the United Nations in New York.

- Offering a session on humanism at the 2013 'Over 60s Festival' in Portsmouth. 34 people booked a place ... over 20 turned up!

- Officiating at the International Humanist Congress in Oxford, at which humanists arrived from many parts of the world, and especially Norway. Listening to humanist choirs from London and Manchester brought tears to my eyes.

- Writing this Handbook – the final draft started on Darwin Day.

How about your experiences through the years? I think we should be told!

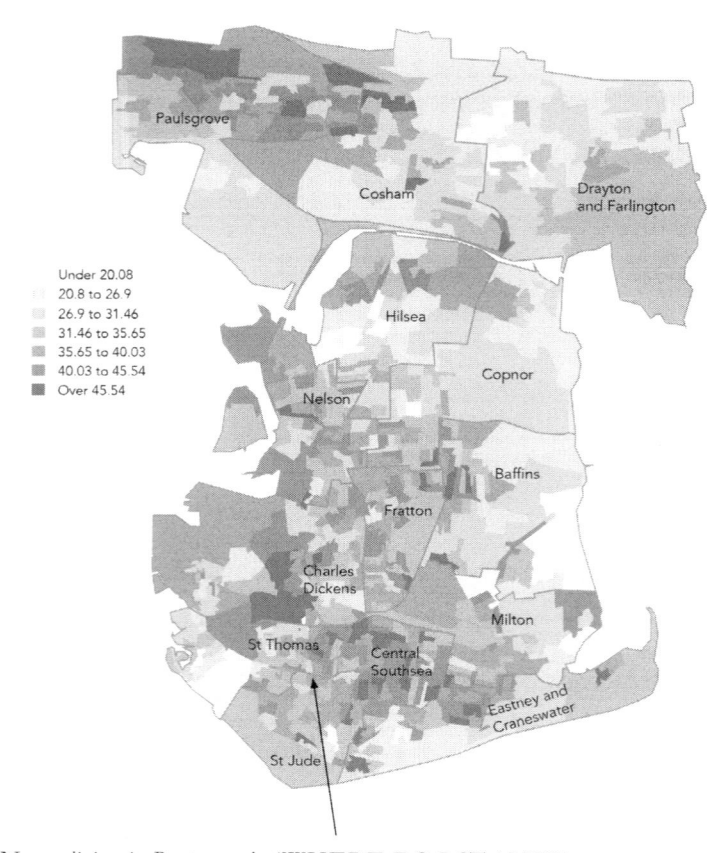

Non-religion in Portsmouth. 'WHERE DO I STAND?'

CHAPTER 3
A QUIVER OF QUOTES, QUICK-WITTED COMMENTS, AND QUIPS:

> An ever-rising 'silver tsunami' of old people.
> Martin Amis

a) *Ageing and Old Age*

1. Diversity of older people

- Ageing faces, ageing bodies, as we know, are endlessly diverse. Lynne Segal

- Five distinct 'identity types' are used in the print media. Older people are 'victims'; 'frail, infirm and vulnerable'; 'radicalised citizens'; 'deserving old'; and 'undeserving old'. Fealey, Mc Namara, Pearl and Lyons

- Age stereotyping results in the association of certain characteristics with certain ages. The effect of this is to apply blanket generalisations to a particular age group and, importantly, 'homogenise' the group, rather than recognising its diversity. Robinson, Gustafson and Popovich

- There is no time within the human lifecycle that there is greater variability between individuals than there is in ageing. Elizabeth MacKinley

- Older people from minority ethnic groups, despite scoring lower on indices of quality of life, such as income, housing and environment, scored higher on indices of community and belonging than the indigenous older population. Peter Coleman

- Old people include some of the fittest, and some of the most decrepit, some of the richest and some of the most powerful, as well as the poorest and most marginalised in any society. Pat Thane

- I'm 80 – in my own mind, my age varies. When I'm performing on stage, I'm 40. When I'm shopping in Waitrose I'm 120. Humphrey Lyttleton

- I told the people of Northern Ireland that I was an atheist. A woman in the audience stood up and said – 'Yes, but is it the God of the Catholics or the God of the Protestants that you don't believe in?'. Quentin Crisp

- We're no longer lumping senior citizens as pensioners together. Instead we are dividing them into catagories. 'Smarties', (senior market town retirees); 'Diamond Dogs', (affluent mortgage-free suburbanites; also 'Grey Panthers', 'Silver Surfers'; 'Twirlies', (too early for bus pass use) 'Solbios', (seniors outside Lidl before it opens).

- The religious experience of the present cohort of elderly people is different from that of the coming generation. Elizabeth MacKinley

2. Characteristics of old age and aging

Apparently greed is a common trait among the very old.

When I hobble onto the stage these days ... I open my set ... with Hoagy Carmichael's Old Rockin' Chair.

In my late seventies I am able to play at senility, enjoying supportive friends, singing, albeit seated and wearing an eye patch, drinking Irish whiskey, fly fishing for trout, looking at works of art and listening to Bessie Smith, the empress of the Blues.

George Melly

- I had thought of old age as a place we all eventually end up – not as the final step in a gradual process of ageing. Sue Ellen Semple

- Everyday every one of us replaces billions of cells. What is remarkable is not that we age, but that we stay young as long as we do. Steve Jones

- It is possible to surmise that those who have little contact with older people will be more influenced by the images portrayed in the media. One study identified eight negative stereotypes. These were eccentrics, curmudgeons) grouchy, angry, uncooperative, nosey/peeping toms), objects of ridicule or the brunt of the joke, unattractive, overly affectionate or sentimental, out of touch with current/modern society, overly conservative, and afflicted (physically or mentally deficient. Schmidt and Boland quoted by Malcolm Sargent

- *Prisoners of Space*, a book which explores the spatial constriction of the lives of older people with advancing years. Five older people living in a working class, inner city urban neighbourhood are asked about places and spaces in their environment. There is Stan's 'stoic resignation', Marie's 'aggressive defiance', Raymond's 'jovial acceptance', Evelyn's 'placid equanimity', and Edward's 'calm accommodation'. The subtle nuances of their geographical experience are striking. Graham Rowles

- Over sixty fives are a net contributor to society (in the UK) at a rate of 30 to 40 billion pounds a year because they pay taxes, spend money that creates jobs, and are volunteers, carers and significant contributors to charity. Lynne Segal quoting Yvonne Roberts

- One can think of old age as a kind of 'natural monastery' in which earlier roles, attachments, and pleasures are stripped away. Elizabeth MacKinley quoting Moody

- Senility, like drunkenness, bothers beholders more than bearers. John Updike

- Like everyone who makes the mistake of getting older: I begin each day with coffee and the obituaries. Bill Crosby

- When an older person dies, it is like a library burning down. Arab proverb

3. Negative aspects of ageing & old age

- As I get older, I find myself more prone to despair. Lucretia Stewart
- Now that I am old, I read very slowly. Charles Darwin
- Above all, old age is associated with loss – loss of a work role, loss of spouse, decreased income and increased physical frailty. Peter Coleman
- Although attitudes to old age vary considerably across time and place, they are rarely free from dread, disgust, and other discriminatory perceptions. Lynne Segal
- When George Bernard Shaw was asked to name the consolations of old age, he remained silent. P. Bristow
- When I was young there was no respect for the young. Now I am old there is no respect for the old. I missed out coming and going. JB Priestley
- Growing old is like being increasingly penalised for a crime you haven't committed. Anthony Powell

4. Positive aspects of ageing & old age

- Media discourses concerning older people contain some positive stereotypes, like old age as the 'golden years of a leisure-filled existence. Nussbaum & Coupland, quoted by Fealey
- At the most basic level, our sense of wellbeing begins simply with what anthropologist Daniel Miller sums up as 'the comfort of things'. Material objects and the delight found in them, joyful association they conjure up for us over a lifetime. Lynne Segal
- Growing old – it's not nice but its interesting. August Strindberg
- Do not regret growing older. It is a privilege denied to many. Anon
- I shall not waste my days in trying to prolong them. Ian Fleming
- Old age, believe me, is a good and pleasant thing. It is true that you are gently shouldered off the stage, but then you are given such a comfortable front row stall as a spectator. Jane Harrison

A CROWN OF COMFORT

THE OLD MAN: "I like this sunshine, my dear, it's a good lot better than the workhouse."
THE OLD LADY: "Yes—thanks to the 5/- a week pension (10/- for the two of us) we old people get through the Act passed by the LIBERALS."

5. Grand children

- Some of us will take pride in surveying the beauty of our children or grandchildren…our genetic stand-in. Grand parenting – keeping our spirits buoyant. Denise Riley
- Elderly parents or grandparents who have little contact with their children are gradually strangled by their lack of affection. How sad that the ties of family affection have been narrowed and loosened in modern society. Nathan Bupp

6. Growing older in place

- The House of Lords is often referred to as Britain's most expensive retirement home. Lewis Wolpert

- Harpenden – full of elderly ladies parking badly. Anna Pavord

- Home is the place you grow up wanting to leave and grow old wanting to get back to. Anon

- Do not leave the place where you lived while working, and where all your friends are, to move to a remote district or the seaside where you know no-one and where most of those living there are even older than you.
Admiral Sir Charles Madden

- Relationships that are based on the comfort of companionship may also be difficult to establish, particularly for those older adults who are dislocated from their known and familiar environments in old age.
Elizabeth MacKinley

- But for many older people the changes within everyday life in their own local communities seemed to have had a more damaging effect on morale. Peter Coleman

- Visitor to old man: *Have you lived here all your life?* Old man: *I don't know, I haven't died yet!* Anon

- In the west, we are entrenched, bolstered by our pensions, brandishing our Freedom Passes, cluttering up the surgeries, with an average life expectancy of around eighty.

- Lifetime is embedded, tethered to certain decades, to places, to people. Penelope Lively

7. Illness and disease

- Ageing is not the enemy. Illness and inactivity are more dangerous. Joyce Brothers

- Stress and ageing – two sides of the same coin. AC Grayling

- Pensioners of the world unite – you have nothing to lose but your pains. Jim Riordan

- Most people, most of the time, find themselves wavering between health and illness, experiencing 'good' days and 'bad' days. The reality of health/illness is much more nuanced and temporarily variable than our readily available discourses allow.
Tia De Nora

- We know that our health and vitality will be short lived, that we will either die young or else wither and become incontinent, arthritic, and repulsive. By giving us something wonderful for a moment, and then gradually pulling it away, we suffer even more than if we had never had it in the first place. Stephan Law

- The hospital years - verdicts delivered by kindly, deliberate consultants; waiting rooms, trolley rides to operating theatres, 'How is your pain today - on a scale of ten?' Penelope Lively

8. Attitudes of seniors

❦ The older you are, the more of your life you have invested as a believer, and if you decide to give it all up a long way into your life, it probably makes you feel a bit daft. Sid Rodrigues

❦ It's harder still to remember to stay open to new ideas as we grow older. That kind of conservatism is hard-wired into the human being. Your skin sags, your organs tire and one day you know for sure that music's not as good as it used to be and that young people need some of whatever it was that made you unhappy as a child. Marcus Brigstocke

❦ As an older man I just find the lead-up to Christmas wearisome. As you get older there are three things you observe: policemen are getting younger. Teenage girls are dressing more like prostitutes. And Christmas comes earlier every year. Ed Byrne

❦ You begin starting listening to any news items containing the word PENSION. Sally Klein

❦ I knew very little about it (old age) until it happened to me. Lord Donald Soper

❦ The old carry around the potential to bore - like a red warning light. Penelope Lively

❦ Bitter old people are an ugly and expressing spectacle, as they fulminate against the degradation of society and the inferiority of young people today. There have been people throughout history who have complained about how everything is going to hell in a handcart, and how ungrateful and undisciplined the new generation is. The rhetoric of irritated abuse is surprisingly consistent down the ages.

❦ *I am not quite over the hill myself, but I have noticed in some of my elderly friends that thier understandable love of the old ways has mutated into an ugly and contemptuous hatred of the new. Given the accelerating rate of change in today's world, it is hardly surprising.*

Richard Holloway

❦ Although no-one wants to go back to the days when Britain ruled the world … the attitude of the old to the world in which they live is still influenced by that memory.

❦ To my surprise and delight, I am rediscovering idealism as I enter my 85th year.

❦ I have become aware as I have got older how little I know. *Tony Benn*

❦ *As I admire a young man who has something of an old man in him, so do I admire an old man who has something of a young man in him.*

❦ *Pomposity and the 'grass is greenerism' are the hallmarks of most old men's pronouncements. Alienating and boring both, no doubt.*

❦ *Who wants to live till they are 98 anyway? Why someone of 97 of course.*

George Melly

9. Sex in loving relationships and marriage

Professor Steve Jones

- Sex and death are close relatives. The gene that makes men male has the same effect on … the grim reaper (as it does on their ability to run marathons and commit crimes). Testosterone is to blame. Steve Jones

- He said, *I can't remember when we last had sex*. And I said, *Well I can and that's why we ain't doing it*. Roseanne Barr

- 'Drop 'em' was what an acquaintance of mine, a young gay man, reported as a typical greeting when he arrived to work on his old people's ward in Brighton. Lynne Segal

- I have no romantic feelings about age. Either you are interacting at any age or you are not. Katherine Hepburn

- Sex can be fun after eighty, after ninety and after lunch. George Burns

- Just because there is snow on the roof, it doesn't mean the fire has gone out. Ralph Waldo Emerson

- One of the myths of ageing is that sexual needs are either not important or non-existent after fifty or sixty years of age. The longings for a sexual relationship among this group of older adults cannot be dismissed. Elizabeth MacKinley

- We want love and companionship. We expect sexual intimacy and attraction, but also a person we respect enough to envision ourselves growing old with. It's a tall order. Greg Epstein

- How do we avoid becoming Grumpy Old People? Get touchy-feely, try being kind to each other, cuddle and say sorry, don't be silent, be silly. *The Guardian*

- An archaeologist is the best husband a woman can have: the older she gets, the more interested he is in her. Agatha Christie

- I still enjoy sex at 74 – I live at 75, so it's no distance. Bob Monkhouse

- I remember with pleasure a sign outside a Rotterdam 'porn' cinema: *Old age pensioner couples half price before 5pm*. Richard Hoggart

- A survey of pensioners in 2006 were asked what in their lives they would change if they could have their time again. 1/5th would have married a different spouse, and 3/4 would have had more sex. Lewis Wolpert

10. Retirement

- There is no affirming ritual that welcomes an older adult into another life stage – that of later life. At best any rituals are closures, such as retirement parties and dinners, perhaps having to give up a driving licence due to failing sight or other disabilities. Events such as fiftieth wedding anniversaries and birthdays are held to recognize the years gone rather than to make new beginnings. *Elizabeth MacKinley*

- The idea of a short retirement as a kind of ultimate holiday with pay. Along with a nice little bungalow outside Morecambe, or a little allotment near Chesterfield, has vanished. Eric Midwinter

- Retirement? Twice as much husband, half as much pay! Annie Wilks

11. Key to successful ageing and longevity

> If you rest...
> you rust
> Helen Hayes

- Remain youthful in spirit, by loving, giving and caring. Dave Brubeck

- We need old friends to help us grow old and new friends to help us stay young. Letty Pogrebin

- As long as we live, there is never enough singing. Martin Luther King

- We may not be trams driven along the lines ordained by supernatural forces of fate or providence, but we are certainly conveyed, often unwittingly along the routes sign posted by our cultural values. We must build a new tram and then decide in which direction to lay its lines. Eric Midwinter

- If I had known I was going to live this long, I would have taken better care of myself. Eubie Blake

- Anyone who keeps the ability to see beauty never grows old. Franz Kafka

- Police in Norway stopped Sigrid Krohn de Lange running down the street in Bergen because they thought she had escaped from a nursing home. The 94 year old jogger was out keeping fit. Newspaper report

- Tango dancing reduces the risk of Alzheimers disease by 75%. Newspaper headline

- Some people use their energy to live many lifetimes in one lifetime. Others, through timidity or lack of imagination use up a whole lifetime living less than one lifetime. Phil Zuckerman

'Who wants to get to the age of 90?'
'Why me of course, I'm 89!'

RMB

Politics and pensions

Who is this pre historic man and what are his beliefs?

Melesse in Addis Ababa

Miss Elsie Greene

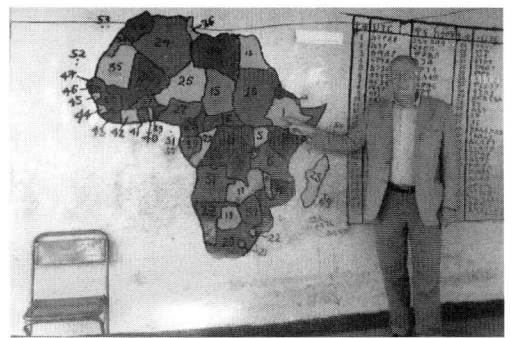

Older people in Ethiopia - many rely on strong coffee and faith to keep them going

12. Politics

✤ In every civilisation there have always been two flames burning, the flame of anger against injustice and the flame of hope that one can build a better world. The best thing the old can do is to fan both flames. Tony Benn

✤ I'm fed up to the ears with old men dreaming up wars for young men to die in. George McGovern

✤ I've become more revolutionary every year I've lived. Trevor Huddlestone

✤ The AARP - the 800 pounds gorilla - the most powerful lobby on Capital Hill. Anon

✤ On 24th October 2012, Mamana Bibu, a 65-year old woman picking vegetables in her family's land in Norther Waziristan, Pakistan was killed by a U.S. drone attack. She was not a terrorist, but a midwife, yet she was blown to pieces in front of her nine grandchildren. News Report

✤ In the UK, we saw repeated scapegoating of the older generation, now mockingly labelled the 'baby boomers' as responsible for all the woes of young people ...

13. Reminiscence

✤ Incitement of resentment of the young towards the old has become yet another repetitive feature of much of the media's channelling of discontent away from any more useful attempt to grapple with the far more complicated analysis of the socially destructive effects of the deregulation of corporate finance and its impact on the problems of nation states.

✤ Ageing is not simply linear ... no ... in our minds we race around, moving seamlessly between childhood, old age, and back again.

✤ Old age no longer appears as simply a type of foreign country separated from the rest of life. *Lynne Segal*

✤ Since Penelope Noakes of Duppas Hill is gone, no-one will ever call me Nelly again. Richard Hoggart

✤ As we grow older, we may become ashamed of our past, we may reflect on wasted years, spot mistaken turnings, recognise occasions when we failed to stand up for what we believed. *Peter Cave*

✤ Life is lived forwards but understood backwards. Soren Kierkegard

✤ I have appeared for over thirty years at Ronnie Scott's, that is to say over a third of my life, covering my involuntary arrival in the suburbs of old age and fairly soon, I fear, the city centre itself.

✤ I feel pretty good. I've a rich memory bank to draw on and I don't care too much what happened yesterday afternoon. *George Melly*

✤ In a dream you are never 80. *Ann Sexton*

✤ I like being old at least as much as I liked being middle aged and a good deal more than being young. Jane Miller

✤ Life is a moderately good play with a badly written third act. Truman Capote

✤ The older a man gets the longer he had to walk to school as a boy. *Henry Brighton*

✤ We old talk too much about the past - this should take place only between consenting contemporaries.

✤ We are all palimpsests.

✤ The world is full of windows. Penelope Lively

14. Humour

- Laugh up to 15 times a day, and you live up to 8 times longer. Sally Brown
- As I grow older and totter to my tomb, I find I care less who goes to bed with whom. Dorothy Sayers
- Pop a few pearls of wit and wisdom everyday and that telegram from Her Majesty is practically in the bag. You see (s)he who laughs, lasts. Rosemary Jarski
- Perhaps a sense of humour is really needed to enable older people to deal with some of the difficulties they encounter in ageing. Elizabeth MacKinley
- Ancestor worship must be an appealing idea to those who are about to become ancestors. Steven Pinker
- Old gardeners never die, they just spade away and throw in the trowel. Herbert Prochnow

15. Longevity

- Anyone who keeps the ability to see beauty, never grows old. Franz Kafka
- Like anybody I would like to lead a long life. Longevity has its place. But I'm not concerned about that now … I have seen the promised land. Martin Luther King

---

- Nowadays, assuming 65 is the age of retirement, a typical pensioner, analysed over the globe as a whole, has about two weeks in which to enjoy his or her gold (or plastic) watch. By 2300 he or she will have, if the UN is justified in its optimism, thirty years.
- Glasgow has the lowest male life expectancy of any city in western Europe, and it is getting worse. In (inner city) Calton men die 28 years younger than in affluent Lenzie – five miles away.
- The life expectancy of the least educated white Americans has dropped by 4 years in the past two decades. In Florida some 70% of men and 50% of women are obese.
- Men are struck by thunderbolts at three times the rate of women, in part because they sometimes stand on golf courses with lightning conductors in their hands.
- God offered comfort to Job … Thou shalt come to thy grave in a full age … for the first time in history, that solace is available to almost all of us.

Steve Jones

- An average human life is less than a thousand months long. One third of those months are spent asleep. AC Grayling
- How old would you be if you didn't know how old you were? Leroy Paige

b) Religion

1. Characteristics

- I know lots of Christians. They're nice, they're fun, they're witty, they're clever, they wear jumpers and eat yoghurt.

- Religion has its past, good, bad ... and inspiring, but what is the future for a system of thought so resistant to change that even a new cover on a hymn book is enough to spark a civil war? Where can religion go from here?

- On the shoulders of the kindest, best-intentioned, gentle believers stand row upon row of increasingly nasty people with 'unquestionable' ethics, ancient books, which they 'know' to be true.

- Jesus seems to have been very charismatic, a good speaker, something of a hippy, which I like, and almost certainly a socialist. *Marcus Brigstocke*

- Often, the cost of your entry ticket to a particular system of belief is to shun certain items (of food) altogether or to obey rigid laws about how they should be prepared. Steve Jones

- Religion is regarded by the common people as true, by the wise as false, and by the rulers as useful. Seneca

- *Acts of God* - a legally recognisable definition meaning the operation of uncontrollable natural forces. Oxford English Dictionary

- Religion is at its best when it helps us to ask questions and holds us in a state of wonder – and arguably at its worst when it tries to answer them authoritatively and dogmatically. Karen Armstrong

- Christianity has a genius for appropriating elements of other people's traditions, which it then stitches into a patchwork pattern of its own devising. Richard Holloway

- We take it that when people talk of God, they are talking of a supreme immaterial being, all powerful, all good and all knowing, standing in some continuing personal relationship with humans. Deists are more austere, believing God to be little more than a creator-designer. Peter Cave

- Another view promoted by liberal Protestant theologians is that God should not be viewed as a supernatural entity outside of space and time, but as a being existing everywhere and every place in space and time. Victor Stenger

- Beliefs about the nature of humankind, its purpose and destiny, and its relationship with the world and universe in which I is embedded, are increasingly referred to as spiritual beliefs. Use of the word 'spiritual' appears to have lost its original tethering alongside religion and to come to a search for connection with and/or belonging to whatever powers, forces or principles are considered to underlie the universe we live in.
  Peter Coleman

- I am in search of God. Where is he? Within you said the conjurer, within me too. George Bernard Shaw

- There is a vague willingness to suppose that there is 'something out there', accompanied by an unsurprising disinclination to spend any time and effort worshipping whatever that might be. Voas and Crockett

- It is a test of a good religion whether or not you can joke about it. GK Chesterton

- These figures are shocking. Three quarters of the American population literally believe in religious miracles ... in the resurrection. It's astounding. These numbers aren't duplicated anywhere in the industrial world. You have to go to mosques in Iran or do a poll among old ladies in Sicily to get numbers like his. Avram Chomsky

- But what about religious behaviour? Why do humans fast, genuflect, self-flagellate, nod manically towards a wall, crusade, or indulge in costly practices that can consume life, and in extreme cases terminate it? Richard Dawkins

- When one guy sees an invisible man, he is a nut case. Ten people see him, it's a cult. 10 million people see him, it's a respected religion. Richard Jeni

- Is man one of God's blunders, or is God one of man's blunders? Friedrich Nietzsche

- When I found out God was white, I lost interest. Alice Walker

- Religion, as a system of beliefs about the existence of God ... I regard as a private matter. So long as I am not requested to give it any public support or affirmation, I have no more desire to expose, refute, or confound it than I do my neighbour's belief that his wife is the most beautiful woman in the world. Sidney Hook

- The majority are content to stick in this position. They accept the religious establishment, as they accept the Monarchy and the Lord Mayor's show. It is colourful and they are used to it. Hector Hawton

- Religion is treated like a senile relative whose bizarre statements are not to be questioned. Walter Sinnott-Armstrong

- Although religionists have every right to express their point of view in the public square, religion should be primarily a private matter. Nathan Bupp

- No matter how they answer the God question, generous-minded people could profit from adopting an attitude of critical sympathy towards religion and maybe even taking the odd dip into it – provided they heed Canon William Vanstone's warning that the Church is like a public swimming pool, where most of the noise comes from the shallow end. Richard Holloway

Religion appears to me like a human pyramid. In Christianity, the impressive triangle of power looks like this. On the bottom, with their feet on the ground are the rank-and-file believer, churchgoers who occasionally arrange flowers and dabble in light charity work. They are not judgemental or mean or smug, and their faith is as honest, as it can be under the circumstances. They enjoy *Thought for the Day* on Radio 4 but like it best when it's a Christian one. One row above them are the ones who are mildly disapproving of the somewhat occasional attendance of the bottom row. The second tier are religiously observant. They pray, sing, attend church, run weekend bible studies, and read *The Daily Mail* without laughing. Above them are

Church scenes

When these two ladybird books were purchased at a charity shop, the sales asssitant was heard to ask her manager - Shall I clasify these under Fiction or non-fiction!?

39

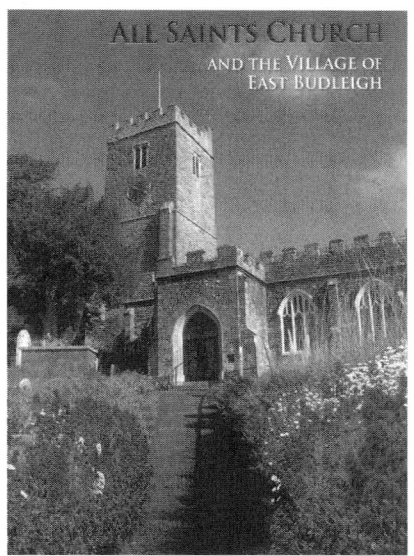

the 'active' members of the Church; they ruthlessly promote their passion for the Christian way of life and would not be the slightest bit abashed to make it clear that Muslims have got it wrong and will go to hell, as will atheists, but not as fast as the Muslims.

Above them, very near the top, are the ones who say, like Stephen Green from Christian voice did, that the floods in New Orleans were God's just punishment for homosexuality. On the shoulders are the violent few willing to kill for God.

The same system works in all the faiths. Bottom-rung ordinary Muslims, praying to Mecca, and trying to be good, carry on their shoulders teetotal, wife-hiding, bearded zealots. Above them are the livid US flag-burning, madressa-educated, evolution-denying nutters, who in turn bear the weight of the Islamists, who find an educated woman an insult to Allah and praise the idea of violent jihad. Teetering on the top are the likes of Al Quaida and their brothers around the globe.

If the bottom rung walked away and decided that with or without faith the religion they belong to was too corroded by power, then the whole ugly mess would begin to crumble. Where would Hezbollah recruit from if most Muslims decided that any connection to the violent political power of Islam was not for them? Where would Israeli Jews find the justification to treat Palestinians like so many of them do? Would Christians succeed in quietly persecuting women and gays?

Marcus Brigstocke

Sometimes we Christians are too polite, too nice, too reasonable, too obedient for our own good. Carey and Carey

---

- Tentatively, I propose to define religions as social systems whose participants avow belief in a supernatural agent or agents whose approval is sought. The definition is subject to revision, a place to start, not something carved in stone to be defended to death. According to this definition a devout Elvis Presley fan club is not a religion, because, although the members may, in a fairly obvious sense, worship Elvis. He is not deemed by them literally supernatural, but just to have been a particularly superb human being.

- Wolfe notes without irony some of the concessions they (religious leaders) are willing to make to contemporary secular culture, concessions that go far beyond web sites and multi-million dollar television programs, or the introduction of electric guitars, drums, and Powerpoint in their services. More attention is paid to providing plenty of free parking and babysitting than to the proper interpretation of passages of scripture. The image they are trying hard to shed is 'Churchianity'. *Blackford and Schlülenk*

2. Diversity

- The church has gone from harshness to happy hymns, from Savonarola to snappy sermons, from punishment to the persuasion of marketing ploys. AC Grayling

- My own religious practices as a Quaker are extremely private. Unmoulded by liturgy, sacraments or priesthood. If there is a God, he is a mountain which will look slightly different to each, according to how we stand at the foot of it, and it can be climbed by many different routes.' Gerald Priestland

- The success of religions depends on their ability to stay distinct from their rivals. Steve Jones

- If you have two religions in your land, the two will cut each other's throats, but if you have thirty religions, they will dwell in peace. Anon

- Religious respondents say they have a religion, believe in God (if only sometimes), and attend services at least monthly. The 'un-religious' have/do none of these things. In between are the 'fuzzy faithful', who identify, believe or attend singly or in some combination, but not all three. In the 2008 British Social Attitudes survey 36% of white respondents are unreligious, 40% fuzzy and 24% religious. Voas and McAndrew

- On a scale of one to seven – one is utter certainty that there is a God and seven utter certainty that there is no such thing. Richard Dawkins

- But Marge, what if we choose the wrong religion. Each week we just made God madder and madder. Homer Simpson

- As a back of the envelope calculation, we can safely say over the past 10,000 years of history, humans have created about 10,000 different religions and about 1000 gods. Blackford and Schüklenk)

- As human culture grew, and people became more reflective, folk religion became transformed into organised religion. Daniel Dennett

- Leicester atheists are more pious than Shropshire Anglicans. Anon

---

- *That makes six gods that I have seen or heard of in my search but none of them is the God I seek,* said the black girl. *Are you in search of God?* Said the first gentleman. *Had you not better be content with mumbo jumbo, or whatever you call the god in your tribe? You will not find any of ours an improvement on him. (The Adventures of a black girl in search for God)* George Bernard Shaw

---

- You see parents in a suburb in the United Kingdom, spitting and throwing stones and hurling abuse at little children on the way to school, because they belong, not even to a different religion but merely to a different sect. This is Christians shouting and spitting at Christians. Philip Pullman

3. Function and role

✤ Parish Priests, like drains, are most likely to be noticed when they go wrong. They hardly attract attention so long as they turn up as required to take Sunday sermons; bury; baptise; and betrothe; refrain from molesting or assaulting parishioners and in old age depart the ministry with good grace to make way for a younger man to continue the cycle. Mathews Parris

✤ Every religion consists of rites, rituals, prayers, social institutions, holidays, etc., and these serve a wide variety of purposes, conscious or otherwise. Sam Harris

✤ Most accounts of the origins of religion amount to one of the following suggestions – human minds demand explanations, human ears seek comfort, human societies require order, and human intellect is illusion prone. Pascal Boyer

✤ The choice of a church wedding (or christening or funeral) by people who do not otherwise attend, seems motivated less by an urge to be briefly religious than by a quest for solemnity, tinged with nostalgia. Steve Bruce

✤ This acknowledges the point that religion....can give comfort and inspiration, and prompt many acts of benevolence…and of course unaccountable acts of benevolence are performed by non- believers too, perhaps more admirably since humanity is the impulse. AC Grayling

✤ Religion and faith among older people effectively offers a sense of meaning, control and self esteem, and helps in the coping with the stresses of old age. Lewis Wolpert

✤ For the greater part of humankind religion continues to provide more satisfying explanations for issues affecting the perceived meaning and purpose of life, which science does not address. Peter Coleman

✤ Christians are still to be found in the worst places on earth, trying to make a difference to the lives of the wretched. It is in its work of organised care for others…. that Christianity is at its most compelling. Secularity is at a disadvantage here. Because it is diffused throughout society…there is no obvious agency that can gather the godless together to motivate them for the work…once a week to be ethically challenged and spiritually uplifted. R Hall

✤ It would certainly be wrong to take away the religious consolation of anyone who was bereaved or ill or old or dying. But people in normal health are a different matter. Barbara Stoke

✤ Religions exist and survive, and continue to flourish even in an era of abundance and science for one profound and irreducible reason: because they are the stories we need. As such, they are by definition the best, and most resonant, the most powerful stories ever told. Thor and Odin; Hercules and Zeus; Adam and Eve; Shiva and Radna; Buddha sitting under the tree; Noah and the Ark….- damned good yarns, each and every one of them, and they influence us all, whether we 'believe' in them or not. Baddiel and David

- ✤ If religion were to alter itself or begin to take a back seat in the affairs of men and women, what might be preserving? Desmond Tutu, I would hope. Architecture, art, music, sculpture, and literature, of course. Only a cultural vandal or a fool would seek to destroy any of those things or to downplay the contribution some aspects of religion have made to our culture.
- ✤ Religion plays a vital role in community. We need each other, we need contact, fellowship and to know that we are not totally alone. The church, mosque, and temple bring people together. What they do when they assemble may not meet with everyone's approval, but the act of assembly is important.
- ✤ The Natural History Museum in London also brings people together. They stand in awe before the wondrous collection of exhibits seeking to further our understanding of the world we share, and eat a slice of rather good cafeteria carrot cake. But is it communion? In a sense I think it is. But it's unstructured compared with religious assembly and no-one would notice if you didn't turn up. There are many other places where we get together – swingers' parties, pubic swimming pools and Marks and Spencer's to name but three – but with the exception of organised clubs and societies, which go some way towards genuine community, none of these places meets the duality of coming together like religion does.

Marcus Brigstocke

- ✤ Who maps it out?....the one above....So God maps it out?...yes, yes. He's got it all worked out. Interviewee cited by Coleman
- ✤ If you meet anyone who tells you his or her religion can offer all the answers, run for the hills, or at least, hide your wallet. Greg Epstein
- ✤ War is God's way of teaching us geography. Paul Rodriguez
- ✤ I'm not an atheist but a kind of agnostic. Religious stuff and church services don't do anything for me. Tanni Grey-Thompson
- ✤ Viewed from a humanist perspective, religion is seen as a strand in the tapestry of human development from primitive society to modern times. Hector Hawton
- ✤ Apparently in her world, God gets the credit if the outcome is good, but takes no responsibility if it's bad. We expect our politicians to behave like that, but God? Louise Antony

- ✤ People may well love religion independently of the benefits it provides them. (I am delighted to learn that red wine in moderation is good for my health, since, whether or not it is good for me, I like it, and I want to go on drinking it. Religion could be like that.) It is not surprising that religion survives. It has been pruned and revised and edited for thousands of years, with millions of variants extinguished in the process, so it has plenty of features that appeal to people...features that ward off or confound enemies and competitors, and secure allegiance.
- ✤ Sociological studies of religion show how successful religions grow not so much by convincing new adherents of doctrinal truth, but by meeting social and psychological needs.

Blackford and Schüklenk

✤ Religions will continue with us into the foreseeable future, and will not simply wither away. They have performed important functions and cannot easily be dismissed.
Nathan Bupp

✤ Religion can lead people out of cycles of poverty and dependency just as it led Moses out of Egypt. Wolfe

✤ Always believe in God. There are some questions Google can't answer. Joke website

✤ In the past, men inherited their faith and were indoctrinated with the faith of a particular community and time and place. A number of human needs led men to imagine and create beliefs, doctrines and myths of the religions of primitive peoples and of more developed civilizations. The need for some explanation of creation, of the origin and purpose of life; the need for believing that they could tap some source of power for survival and reproduction and fertility; and the need for some belief about death – those evoked the religious life of every community. Paul Kurtz

"Songs of Praise" to celebrate the International Day of Older People

Friday 30th September 2016
St Mary's Church, Fratton Road
From 1.30pm
Advice and information from organisations working with older people
Favourite hymns
Tea and cake
All welcome!

✤ Most accounts of the origins of religion amount to one of the following suggestions – human minds demand explanations, human hearts seek comfort, human societies require order, and human intellect is illusion prone.
Pascal Boyer

✤ It seems that to some women – but not men – church-going was a consolation for a solitary life. Peter Townsend

✤ I see religion as an art form. Ever since we fell out of the trees and became recognisably human, we created religion and works of art to give us some sense that life has ultimate meaning and value to make us wonder, to hold us in an attitude of awe, because we're meaning-seeking creatures.

✤ The weather does lots of different things and so does religion.

✤ We look for ecstasy, and if we don't find in a church or synagogue or a mosque, we'll look for it in rock music, in theatre, music, drugs, sex, skiing even, sport, because we feel then, we are living most fully.

✤ Religion was never supposed to provide answers to questions that lay within the reach of human reason. Religion's task, closely allied to that of art, was to help us to live creatively, peacefully and even joyously with realities for which there were no easy explanations and problems that we could not solve: mortality, pain, grief, despair, and outrage at the injustice and cruelty of life. Over the centuries people in all cultures discovered … and experienced a transcendence that enabled them to affirm their suffering with serenity and courage. *Karen Armstrong*

✤ Every religion offers a comprehensive, coherent, simple, accessible and pleasing theory of the universe and our place in it. To most humans science is cold, distant and offers no emotion gratification, while religion is warm and consoling. *Jacques Monod*

✤ We need to understand what makes religions work, so that we can protect ourselves in an informed manner from the circumstances in which religions go haywire.

✤ Perhaps the main reason that religions do most of the heavy lifting in parts of America is that people really do want to help others – and secular organisations have failed to compete with religions for the allegiance of ordinary people.

✤ The three favourite purposes for religion are to comfort us in our suffering and allay our fears of death; explain things that we can't otherwise explain; and to encourage group cooperation in the face of trials and enemies.
Daniel Dennett

✤ My father's faith, I think, had been formed in World War 1, when he was an officer. He saw the good work done by the padres of the time. It was a simple, practical one. It made people feel better. It cheered them up when they were dying. Philip Pullman

> 43% of those aged 68 and over are certain that God exists. *Daily Mail*

4. Demographics

☦ The poor tend to be more religious than the rich, both within and between nations.

☦ It seems extraordinarily unlikely that there is a genetic explanation for the fact that the French, Swedes and Japanese tend not to believe in God while Americans, Saudis, and Somalis do.
Sam Harris

☦ I hope I never get so old that I get religion. Ingmar Bergman

☦ The gender differences in church congregations is also partly explained by the greater number of older women than older men in the population as a whole. Peter Coleman

☦ Since I got to 80, I've started to read the bible a lot more. It's like kind of cramming for my finals. Vincent Watson

☦ The church regards the elderly as the enduring backbone of their dwindling congregations. The Observer

☦ Christians are more obsessed with gay people than gay people are, and that is saying something. Marcus Brigstocke

☦ In country after country the pattern is the same: religious traditionalists bring forth their baskets and quivers of progeny. Meanwhile birth rates among more secular populations are stagnating or declining. Jacques Berlinerblau

☦ People apparently either choose partners with the same religious views or they switch, acquire or lose religion to accommodate their spouses.

☦ Women are more religious on average than men in nearly all places and periods. In relation to the strong association between (adult) age and religiosity a growing body of research suggests ... this is not because individuals become more religious as they grow older, rather because each successive generation is less religious than the one before it.

☦ Attendance at religious services is substantially higher among graduates than non-graduates at all ages.

☦ Several million people live in this unbuckled 'British Bible Belt' in the north west and north east regions of England.

☦ The final puzzle is why there is so much local variation in the prevalence of religious identity, even when we control for age, sex, and ethnicity. On the face of it, some parts of the country are as religious as Ireland, where 94% reported a religious affiliation in the 2006 Census, and other parts approach the secularity of East Germany, where 74% reported no religious affiliation in 2008.

Voas and McAndrew

5. Sex

- A lot of truly harmless, pleasurable sexual activities that adults could reasonably enjoy are frowned upon or even prohibited in many part of the world, because of church interventions. Udo Schüklenk

- Almost every sexual impulse has been made the occasion for prohibition, guilt, and shame by religions - manual sex, oral sex, anal sex, and non missionary position sex. Christopher Hitchens

- Religion is also to be blamed for the hideous consequences of the masturbation taboo. For decades, millions of young men and boys were terrified in adolescence by supposedly 'medical' advice that warned them of blindness, nervous collapse, and descent into insanity if they resorted to self gratification. Robert Baden-Powell composed an entire obsessive treatise on the subject, which he used to reinforce the muscular Christianity of his Boy Scout movement. To this day, the madness persists on Islamic Web sites purporting to offer counsel to the young. AC Grayling

- Religion has involved itself in issues of sex with both theory and practical exams. It has failed and needs a re-sit. Marcus Brigstocke

- Tuscans refer to the missionary position as the 'Angelic' position. It is also referred to as the 'Mama-Papa' position.

- I had sex with a Christian charity worker in the missionary position. I have had many roles in the church, but being a missionary is not my favourite position. *Sik website*

- The Rev John White, a former Royal Navy chaplain was … after he presented himself at his bedroom window stark naked to a plain clothes policewoman. His defence: 'He always did that sort of thing in the Navy', did not find favour.

- In 1959 Rev. Hopkins Evans told his wife he was going to watch a cricket match but instead went to Hyde Park to look at courting couples through binoculars. He was fined £2 by Marlborough Magistrates Court. Matthew Parris

- It is quite lawful for a Catholic woman to avoid pregnancy by resorting to maths, though she is strictly forbidden to resort to physics or chemistry. HL Mencken

- In 1854 Pope Pius IX issued a Bull that lifted the taint of copulation from the holy child's mother.

- The Catholic church still has a convoluted connection with the marital bed, and what it accepts as 'natural' (and hence acceptable). The rhythm method is accepted by the Catholic church for married couples. But as the technique has a high failure rate a steady influx of candidates for baptism is guaranteed.

- Across the entire globe the devout, of whatever their denomination, are almost always more fertile than their secular neighbours.

- Clerical celibacy took hold from the 4th century, and the Vatican enjoins its acolytes to avoid sex 'for the sake of the kingdom of heaven'.

- The bible of 1631 omits the word 'Not' from the seventh commandment – which then reads, with some optimism – 'Thou shalt commit adultery'. *Steve Jones*

Can you tell me the way to Conway Hall?

Yes

Turn right at the church

Go past the synagogue

Then left at the mosque

Then go to the far corner of Red Lion Square

TT

9. Missionaries

- I've no time for Mother Teresa at all. My impression ... is that while she showed great compassion for the dying poor of India she showed no interest at all in the conditions which had made them poor in the first place. George Melly

- During the Irish potato famine, anti Catholic missionaries from England offered food to anyone who would convert ... but most of the locals chose to suffer instead. Steve Jones

- We are not trying to convert at this stage of life. Comment by a hospital chaplain

- When the white missionaries came to Africa they had the bible and we had the land. They said 'Let us pray.' We closed our eyes. When we opened them we had the bible and they had the land. Desmond Tutu

- Missionaries are perfect nuisances and leave every place worse than they found it. Charles Dickens

- Mother Theresa did much during her long life to alleviate the sufferings of the diseased, deprived and dying, but it seems never to have occurred to her that by accepting contraception she would have found fewer on the streets (of Calcutta) in need of succour. Ludovic Kennedy

10a. Church of England

✢ Anglican atheists – people found wandering around the ruins of the Church of England. George Orwell

✢ We can be critical of the ideology behind Islam as well as the way in which it is sometimes practised without being critical of those who belief in Allah or attend a mosque. Alom Shaha

✢ C of E will, by 2031, be reduced to a 'trivial voluntary association with a large portfolio of heritage properties'. Steve Bruce

✢ Revolution doesn't tie in with the Church of England. Think of a nice, tasteful evensong in the parish church. Very good ladies going in and arranging the flowers. They're not interested in revolution. Karen Armstrong

✢ The Church of England is so often in turmoil. It's more progressive than most of the others, which is to say they move at the same pace as a weary snail with a six-bedroom maisonette on its back, but still faster than the rest. Marcus Brigstocke

> C of E Christmas & Easter. *AC Grayling*

✢ I grew up with the bible and the rituals of the Church of England. Penelope Lively

10b. Catholicism

✤ Let's look at it this way: A Catholic who tells a pollster that she is a Catholic is a Catholic. She is the daughter of an age-old organisation with stable beliefs and dogma and mechanisms for promulgating them. She has places to pray, to consult, to dialogue, to query. Catholic places. Places where people recognise one another as Catholics. They do so because the Catholic Church has spent the better part of the past two millennia fashioning people just like them into Catholics with a sense of Catholic identity. Berlinerblau

✤ In his capacity as leader of the wealthiest church on earth, the Pope is able to make lots of interesting visits, particularly to places where there's grinding poverty. Marcus Brigstocke

✤ The De Salle brothers were mainly Irish lads who'd made it out of the bog to become brothers. Joan Bakewell

✤ Geography, not St Patrick is to blame for the lack of snakes in Ireland. *Steve Jones*

✤ If Jesus had been killed twenty years ago, Catholic school children would be wearing little electric chairs around the their necks instead of crosses. *Lenny Bruce*

❧ I moved from Catholicism to Marxism. Terry Eagleton

❧ There are secular Catholics in my family, there are probably some in yours. They constitute the oceanic and silent penumbra of the Catholic Church. Tom Beaudoin

> Catholicism, with its special effects, its stained glass windows and incense, was a little more intriguing. I understood that it aimed to transport its adherents to some alternative dimension above the dull brick surface of Lovell, but in aiming for the transcendent, it managed, for me at least, to achieve only the weird. *Barbara Ehrenreich*

10c. Jewish

❧ Being a Jew can mean many things. It's a faith group and a race (tribe). For some I know being a Jew is a a way of behaving and a preference for certain types of food and little else; for others it's a life sentence. Marcus Brigstocke

❧ Holocaust jokes are not funny. Anne Frankly I wouldn't tolerate them. Joke website

❧ Yes, on the whole I've been annoyed by the Jewish God. I think he's a Victorian, vindictive, capricious, spiteful and, above all, absent more of the time. Jonathan Miller

❧ A secular couple in Tel Aviv in the 1990s produced 2.27 kids, while their ultra-orthodox counterparts brought forth a whopping 7.61 young ones.

❧ A recent poll in the United States indicated that 44% of all 'Jews by religion' surveyed referred to themselves as 'secular' or somewhat 'secular'.

❧ Secular Jew is a familiar cultural trope, deeply ingrained in the popular imagination. Nearly everyone in the United states knows and loves and is perhaps even married to a secular Jew. A variety of images and even stereotypes are associated with this group. They are city dwellers holding advanced degrees. They are comedians and iconoclasts. They are your second grade teacher, Mrs Fantowitz. *Jacques Berlinerblau*

10d. Islam

✤ In today's Arab world it is not religiosity that is mandatory, it's the appearance of it - social hypocrisy provides breathing room to secular life styles.
Ahmed Benchemsi

✤ Most people think that paradise is a fixed place of gardens, rivers, of milk and honey and beautiful women....Part of this is Muslim folklore, part of it is orientalist interpretation. The Muslim paradise is very sophisticated.
Zianddin Sander

✤ I can't remember exactly when I stopped being a Muslim. I suppose people can go through their entire lifetime without questioning a religion they were born into (out of no choice of their own), especially if it doesn't have much say in their lives. If you live in France or Britain, for example, there may never be a need to actively renounce Christianity or come out as an atheist. But when the state sends a 'Hezbollah' (the generic term for Islamist) to your school to ensure that you don't mix with your friends who are boys, stops you from swimming, forces you to be veiled, deems males and females separate and unequal, prescribes different books for you and your girlfriends from those read by boys, denies certain fields of study to you because you are female, then you have no choice but to question, discredit and confront – all of it. Maryam Namazie

✤ *Militant religiosity (fundamentalism) arises where secular, Western-style government have separate religion from politics, and/ or traditional religious beliefs and practices were seen to be under pressure. Islam became radicalised and the mosque was often seen as the only place where people could express their discontent.* Karen Armstrong

✤ The way Moslems worship has a profound and moving devotion to it. The preparation, the washing, and gathering together to face Mecca and literally prostrate oneself before Allah speaks to a passion I wish I could find in myself.

✤ I've heard a few women sing the praises of the jilbab, nikab, burka and all the rest, claiming that the anonymity these garments provide is a relief from the ogling eyes of men. Proof that a person can both flatter and demean themselves in the same thought.

✤ I wonder why Islamists' sincere disgust at atrocity doesn't convince more of them to abandon, if not their faith, then at least some of the structures of Islamic social and political life.

✤ Thank goodness – no one wants to see Hovis the subject of a mental jihad because they accidentally baked a forbidden image into a loaf of malted granary.
Marcus Brigstocke

✤ We can be critical of the ideology behind Islam as well as the way in which it is sometimes practised without being critical of hose who belief in Allah or attend a mosque. Alom Shaha

11. Hypocrisy/ absurdity/ illegality

- A religion without superstition does not deserve the name. Steve Jones

- All religions are founded on the fear of many and the cleverness of the few. Stendahl

- Today, religion is trying its best to utilize many of the inventions, but at the same time it is not open to promoting the scientific outlook. Vikas Gora

- The relevance of the brain's dopaminergic systems to religious experience, belief and behaviour is suggested by several lines of evidence. Sam Harris

- There's a religious slot broadcast every morning on the radio called Thought for the Day, and it's marvellous. Because it usually involves some bishop telling you what he did the day before, and shovelling Jesus into it somehow. Mark Steel

- It's best to read the weather forecast before praying for rain. Mark Twain

- Belief is intellectual surrender; faith is a state of willed self-delusion. *Barbara Ehrenreich*

- Just two words state the objection to faith-based schools: 'Northern Ireland'.

- Do the preachers and prophets also believe, or do they just 'believe in belief'?

- (Frederick) Douglass was somewhat ambivalent about religion, noting… that the most devout Christians made the most savage slave holders.

- All the major conflicts in history, as in the world today, are the product, direct or by legacy, of differences in religious dogma and practice. No-one has ever fought a war because of disagreements in geology or botany.

- Religious apologists are inveterately apt to defend against criticism or refutation by saying, 'That is not what I mean by religion', and 'I don't recognize that caricature of what I believe'. Part of the sleight of hand at work here becomes obvious when one notes the great difference between the ordinary votaries of a religion believe and what their theologians and high priests say. If you speak to a theologian, you will find that, in the complexified and polysyllabic rarifications of his craft, at least not all these things are to be taken literally, but have metaphorical or mystical interpretations, though the grounds on which bits of the story are to be cherry-picked for literal truth and which are to be treated as metaphor are moot.

AC Grayling

- How beautiful that melon is … isn't it proof that Goddy exists?

- And God said 'let there be light', and there was light but the electricity board said he would have to wait until Thursday to be connected. *Spike Milligan*

🕆 Queen Elizabeth told the Catholics and Puritans that she had done her best to make a church that would satisfy both of them; that they must come to it every Sunday or go to prison. She overlooked the fact that there was a third alternative - America.

George Bernard Shaw

🕆 Maybe I'm wrong, but whoever it was that planned dementia, childhood leukaemia, AIDS, cancer, malaria and for BAE system to be one of the UK's biggest exporters needs to take their plan back to their celestial drawing board, and have a think.

🕆 Great music thrives in many Christian churches, but so does illogical, unchallengeable hate, fear, and selected ignorance.

🕆 They all believe in the same God. Jews, Christians, and Muslims all share one God on a sort of aggressive dysfunctional time-share.

🕆 There are some good rules that come from religion. Turning the other cheek seems like a decent idea, though there are only two cheeks to turn so it's still really two strikes and you're out. *Marcus Brigstocke*

🕆 We must respect the other fellow's religion, but only in the sense and to the extent that we respect his theory that his wife is a beauty and his children smart.
HL Mencken quoted by Dawkins

🕆 We are talking far too much about God these days and what we say is often facile ... Surely everybody knows what God is: the Supreme Being, a divine Personality, who created the world and everything in it. They look perplexed if you point out that it is inaccurate to call God the Supreme Being because God is not a being at all, and that we don't know what we mean when we say that he is 'good', 'wise', or 'intelligent'. People of faith know in theory that God is utterly transcendent, but they seem sometimes to assume that they know exactly who 'He' is and what he thinks, loves and expects. We tend to tame and domesticate God's 'otherness'. We regularly ask God to bless our nation, save our queen, cure our sickness or give us a fine day for the picnic ... Politicians quote God to justify their policies; teachers use him to keep order in the classroom; and terrorists commit atrocities in his name. We beg God to support 'our' side in an election or a war, even though our opponents are, presumably, also God's children and the object of his love and care.

🕆 The biblical God is a 'starter kit'; if we have the inclination and ability, we are meant to move on. *Karen Armstrong*

🕆 There is a God-intoxicated chaos of injunctions that vary both between religions and within a single religion, leading to incompatibilities and some downright immoralities parading as moral. *Peter Cave*

- There would be no such churches in the first place if humanity had not been afraid of the weather, the dark, the plague, the eclipse, and all manner of other things now easily explicable. And also if humanity had not been compelled, on pain of extremely agonizing consequences, to pay exorbitant tithes and taxes that raised the imposing edifices of religion.

- Any hospital supervisor in the country will tell you that patients sometimes make astonishing recoveries. Those who desire to certify miracles may wish to say that such recoveries have no 'natural' explanation. But that does not mean that there is therefore a 'supernatural' one.

- Gullibility and credulity are considered undesirable qualities in every department of human life – except religion.

Christopher Hitchens

- Yet only a few prayers are, seemingly, answered. Of the two opposing football teams that both pray for victory, only one can have its wish granted. Of the two conflicting religious forces that both pray for domination, only two, at most, can succeed. Christine Overall

- That's the advantage of Goddy epistemology, of course: it's so extraordinarily flexible, so convenient, so personalised. The knowledge is so neatly moulded to fit individual wishes. God is good when I win and blameless when I lose, good when I survive the tsunami, and out of the equation when other people are swept away and drowned. Ophelia Benson

- It is trite but true, that religion is one of the most divisive of all human enterprises. Quite apart from the wars conducted in its name, is the unlovely assumption of pretty well every religion that they are the only ones to be saved … If I am a Muslim, I know that Christians are infidels. They can't all be right! Sheila McLean

- How many Amish dos it take to change a light bulb? 'What's a light bulb? Joke website

- There's plenty about Christ to enjoy. I'd love to have seen him turn over the tables of the moneylenders in the temple. Direct action and part-time wine making make for a heady combination and an exciting personality. If ever he did come back he'd have a field day on Wall Street. Sadly as a bearded Arab with a history of sedition and religious extremism, he'd stand no chance of getting past security at JFK, let alone coming anywhere near Wall street. Marcus Brigstocke

12. Decline and loss of faith

❧ In the midst of religious crisis in the 1960s, 1970s, 1980s, and 1990s, church people continued to predict a corner about to be turned in church decline. Then, really quite suddenly in 1963, something very profound ruptured the character of the nation and its people, sending organised Christianity on a downward spiral to the margins of social significance. In unprecedented numbers, the British people since the 1960s have stopped going to church, have allowed their church membership to lapse, have stopped marrying in church and have neglected to baptise their children. Meanwhile, their children, the two generations who grew to maturity in the last thirty years of the twentieth century, stopped going to Sunday school, stopped entering confirmation or communicant classes, and rarely, if ever, stepped inside a church to worship in their entire lives.

Nor is it the death of the belief in God, for though that too has declined, it may well remain as a root belief of people. But the culture of Christianity has gone in Britain in the new millennium. Britain is showing the world how religion as we have known it can die. Callum Brown

❧ For most of the 20th century, and not only in the West, organised belief in the supernatural was held to be in decline. All of us know the story. Science, Rationalism, and Materialism – usually personified by the Europeans Darwin and Lyell, Marx and Freud – had given religious belief such a bashing that its explanations of how the world came to be, how we came to be in it, and how we should best live in it, and what would happen to us after death – these explanations and the structures that went with them, became, simply, unbelievable and disagreeable. The idea of God as creator and custodian died … or so the secularists thought, forgetting the great psychologist William James' judgement that beliefs do not work because they are true, but true because they work. Ian Jack

> ❧ Marx, Freud and Weber – along with innumerable anthropologists, sociologists, historians, and psychologists influenced by their work – expected religious belief to wither in the light of modernity. It has not come to pass. Sam Harris

❧ I prayed for twenty years, but received no answer, until I prayed with my legs. Frederick Douglass

❧ Disillusionment appeared to be focussed more on the institutional church than on the idea of God itself. Peter Coleman

❧ We have not lost faith, but we have transferred it from God to the medical profession. George Bernard Shaw

❧ We live in testing yet thrilling times for Christian believers. Carey & Carey

🌿 When I asked first if there was anyone who would describe themselves as having some sort of faith, religion, or perhaps even curiosity about the possibility of something beyond this existence, the hands went up very slowly indeed. Marcus Brigstocke

🌿 Paradoxically religious influence in public life – now at its highest for a generation or more – seems to have risen in inverse proportion to the decline of Christianity.
Keith Porteous Wood

🌿 An external God sitting above the clouds, as represented in popular religion, faces bleak prospects. Behind every pulpit an invisible clock is ticking, counting off the hours as thousands of people flee from churches and temples Deepak Chopra

🌿 I've just checked the Twitter account of Jesus. He is losing followers at an alarming rate. Sikh website

---

🌿 Churches decline because they lose members – by death or defection.

🌿 In July 1950 the bishop of Penrith confirmed 35 candidates, but six only of the newly- confirmed made their first communion on the following Sunday. *Steve Bruce*

---

13. Benefits

🌱 Oxford college chaplains do not seem to believe in anything at all; except, perhaps, good works among the poor in the East End of London. Sir Alfred Ayers

🌱 Of course believing that God exists does not make God exist … Perhaps religions hold societies together, promote flourishing lives and sustain morality. Sometimes the distinctive feature of religion is marked by stressing belief in God, rather than belief that God exists. Peter Cave

🌱 In fact the empirical evidence suggests that health associations with religion, from quicker recovery from physical and mental illness to lowered mortality rates are stronger in older age groups, suggesting an age-related benefit to continued belief. McFadden and Levin

🌱 A widespread belief exists that, even if religion is not true, it is worth practicing because of its benefits. The only definite positive correlation between religious practice and health is with church-going, and it is not proven that this is anything supernatural. It is far more likely to be simply the result of a healthier, less stressful lifestyle among churchgoers. Most non believers I know also live healthy, less stressful lives, but they are never included in these studies. Victor Stenger

🌱 Suppose I can understand the comfort that people of faith might get from the belief that they will live for ever and they will be reunited with their loved ones. *Sheila McLean*

🌱 Those whose beliefs are strongly rooted in Christian doctrine are best able to cope with the onset of old age.
Lord Murton

❧ They … Dawkins and Hitchens are wrong. There is more good religion than bad.

❧ We should teach our children creeds and customs, prohibitions and rituals, texts and music, and when we cover the history of religion, we should include the positive – the role of the churches in the civil rights movement of the 1960s, the flourishing of science and the arts in early Islam, and the role of the Black Muslims in bringing hope, honour and self respect to the otherwise shattered lives of many inmates of our prisons.

❧ In urban and industrial communities too, the draining away of services and resources at periods of economic hardship has meant that the parish priest has been at times a crucial focus for keeping beleaguered neighbourhoods afloat and for breathing into them a vision of new life and worth and purpose. Sometimes the parish priest is the only professional person still living in the area that he or she serves.

❧ Church people are more likely to be committed to serving others than non-churchgoers; they give to charities more than non-churchgoers; they are often to be found abroad serving the very poor of the world, than most non-churchgoers.

❧ In every neighbourhood in Britain the churches are playing some kind of role in building the common good. They maintain buildings that are used by the whole neighbourhood, run parents and toddlers groups, parenting courses, lunch clubs for the elderly, and social events to unite the community. There are many church community centres, youth cubs, advice centres and credit unions. Church buildings now increasingly host post offices and shops for isolated communities. On an everyday basis, clergy and church workers visit the sick and disabled maintaining a link with those who could otherwise become isolated and lonely. *Carey & Carey*

❧ People who are buffeted by the vicissitudes of the economy or who are victimised by injustices, or who are scorned or vilified by the successful members of their societies, or whose work is tedious and unrewarding; people for whom material rewards are scanty, or for whom the toys of consumer culture pall, can unburden themselves most readily in religious settings and find in their church a supportive community. That is why the voices of reason are as sounding brass or as tinkling cymbals. For many Americans their churches … not only provide a sense of hope, illusory to be sure, but also offer other mechanisms of comfort. These are places in which hearts can be opened, common ground with others can be explored, places in which here is a real sense of community, places in which people come to matter to one another – and thus come to matter to themselves. Without such places, what is left? Religious leaders have offered the poor and downtrodden opportunities to reclaim their rights. From the meeting houses that have broadcast the outcry of the urban poor to the liberal Catholic churches of Latin America, religion has provided a place in which individual sufferings can be united in a political movement. At their best the religions of the world have championed the causes of the oppressed. Philip Kitcher

❦ *For students the church provide 'socializing opportunities, forms of care, practical help and spiritual resources'. Religion was carried as a 'portable resource and helped them to cope with the transition to life in higher education'.* Sharma and Guest

❦ *I do, however, appreciate old hymn tunes, coffee mornings, bring and buy sales and a good cathedral.* Anna Pavrod

14. Disadvantages

❦ Violent, irrational, intolerant, allied to racism and tribalism, and bigotry invested in ignorance and hostile to free enquiry, contemptuous of women and coercive towards children: organised religion ought to have a great deal on its conscience. Christopher Hitchens

❦ I found that the people I had most trust in were no longer trustworthy and in fact were evil. I saw minor things such as a person smoking or drinking wine and that of course made me rather cynical. But this person, who was a member of the Church, had molested me. It was so shocking and yet I couldn't say anything because my mother would become upset. Amy Tan

❦ 'Religion has been the cause of all the major wars in history.' This sentence, reiterated like a mantra, by American commentators, psychiatrists, London taxi owners and Oxford academics. Karen Armstrong

❦ None of this is to deny that religion is also capable of doing enormous harm. The history of religions reveals consolations, but also the fanatical intolerance that expresses itself in warfare and persecution, that divides families, cities, and nations, that forbids people to express their love as, and with whom, they choose. Philip Kitcher

❦ You see parents in a suburb in the United Kingdom, spitting and throwing stones and hurling abuse at little children on the way to school, because they belong, not even to a different religion but merely to a different sect. This is Christians shouting and spitting at Christians. Religion is to blame for that. Philip Pullman

❦ Prolonged exposure to the fumes of incense and burning candles may have some detrimental health effect, concluded one recent study. Blackford and Schüklenk

❦ Religiosity is such a waste of time and energy. Millions of men and women in India spend billions of man-hours in religious activities by way of compulsion, profession, or pastime, or simply because they find nothing else to do. TV channels spend millions of precious rupees in praise of god-men who become richer in the process. And so much remains to be done for mankind, for this planet of ours.
Sumitra Padmanasham

❦ Religion to me has always been the wound, not the bandage. Dennis Potter

End of Life

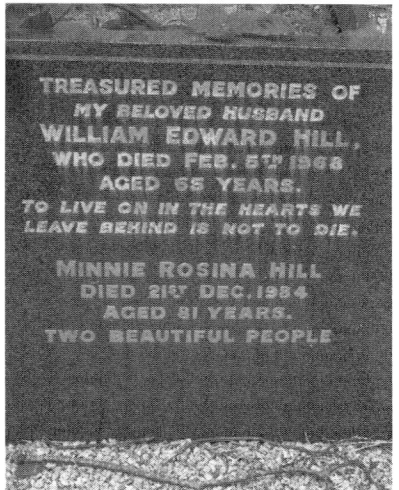

c) End of Life: Death, Dying and the Afterlife

1. Death

- When I wake up in the morning and nothing hurts. I know I must be dead. *George Burns*

- Old age is more to be feared than death. AC Grayling

- I think that the final 'God be with you', the one that comes when we die, is the thing that draws more people to faith than perhaps anything else. Death is the absolute unknown, and even the most ardent thrill-seekers are afraid of it. If they offered 'Actual Death' at Alton towers there'd be no queue. Marcus Brigstocke

- Some old people are oppressed by the fear of death, but an old man who has known human joys and sorrows, and has achieved whatever work it was in him to do, the fear of death is somewhat abject and ignoble. Bertrand Russell

The overwhelming fact of life is its finitude and fragility It passes so quickly. We are each destined to be buried in the sands of time.

- Death is the sound of distant thunder at a picnic. WH Auden

- The death of an 85 years old is likely to attract such phrases as – 'had a good innings', and 'lived to a ripe old age'. Hockey quoted by Moyra Sidell

- We should not see death as an injury, but rather life as a privilege. Barbara Stoker

- Humanists take death to be annihilation. The body remains as a corpse and gradually breaks up, or more swiftly, if enflamed. Peter Cave

- When death is there, we are not; when we are here, death is not. Epicurius

- Darwinian evolutionists recognise that death is final, not simply the death of each individual, but the possible extinction at some day in the remote future of the human species itself. Nathan Bupp

- Looking into the abyss. It's three o'clock in the morning and I can't sleep....I have been invaded by a terrible sense of ultimate meaningless. I have been engulfed by the void, made to look into the abyss of emptiness, extinction, complete nothingness, non-being. Not to be here. Not to be anywhere. My blues in the wee small hours are not caused by the apprehension at the prospect of my own death and extinction, though I hope my number will not be called anytime soon. Richard Holloway

- My father died without having said the words I love you to me. I know he loved me. But I missed him saying the words. Greg Epstein

- **Be happy while you're living, for you're a long time dead.** *Scottish proverb*

- Birth was the death of him. Samuel Becket

- It's life that defeats the Christian church. She is always well equipped to deal with death. Joe Orton

- What a simple thing death is, just as simple as the falling of an autumn leaf. Vincent Van Gogh

- It is likely that most of you have had, or will have your life saved at least once by the new medical technologies ... .

- If children live longer then eventually they die at older ages. Death has been redistributed from the young to the old. *Olshansky and Carnes*

- Most people believe that life ends at death. If you really believed that life goes on after death, you wouldn't put such care as you do in avoiding death. Dying would be like going to bed: a bummer if you're having a good time, but heck, you'll have another good time tomorrow (and if not tomorrow, then the next day, or the next one after that.) You would wish, encourage, hasten the death of the poor, sick, depressed or otherwise worst off, since their next life could only get better. Adele Mercier

- Life's full of danger: as soon as one is born, one is old enough to die. Paul Kurtz

- According to one widely held view, we achieve our immortality in our living presence in the things or persons that continue after our death. We term this view immortality by remembrance. This view also plays a subtle role in our own everyday experience. Craftspeople, writers and artists put something of themselves – their ideas, beliefs, hopes, fears, and views of the world – into their work. They hope their creations will have lasting significance of themselves so that their ideas or fame will long outlive them. Other persons gain immortality by painting on the canvas of history: holding public office, winning or losing battles, revolting against authority, committing outrageous crimes, or making discoveries or inventions. Some obtain their immortality by improving the lives of others, while others seek to prolong their lives in their children, giving their children their own or their forbears' names. *Michael Peterson*

2. Dying

- Most of us … are concerned about how we die, as much as when we die. AC Grayling

- My grandmother is dying at the moment. She is very, very old. You could argue that it's her time. That may be true. Certainly the perverse obsession with the preservation of life, no matter what quality it holds, is one I am horrified by. The real sadness of it all is that it's happening very slowly and each day she survives is not so much a gift from God as a sentence from humanity. When my wonderful grandmother is lucid enough to understand it, she is facing death with an idea an her head. Perhaps a 'hope' would be a better description of what she feels. She's facing the end of her life hoping she'll see my granddad again. Now she is looking forward to seeing him again. I don't know if she will. I don't think so, but I hope she does. Marcus Brigstocke

> - I don't want to achieve immortality through my work. I want to achieve it through not dying.
> - It's not that I'm afraid to die - I just don't want to be here when it happens. *Woody Allen*

- According to Elisabeth Kubler-Ross people's reactions to their own impending death go through stages – denial, anger, 'bargaining' attempting to make some sort of deal either with God or fate for an extension of life, depression/sadness, and acceptance. Moryra Sidell

- My father's faith had been formed in World War 1. He saw the good work done by the padres of the time. It made people feel better. It cheered them up when they were dying. Philip Pulman

- There are so many ways of dying, it's astonishing that any of us choose old age. Beryl Bainbridge

- No matter how unbearably patients suffer due to illness or injury toward the end of their lives, the world's monotheistic religions stand as one in their rejection of many dying patients' requests to end their lives in dignity. … This is surprising, given that at the end of our natural lives churches have promised us that we would be going to heaven - or hell, as the case may be. If at the end of a decently lived life we would go to heaven and enjoy eternal life, why are they fighting our earthly death so vigorously? None of this makes any sense at all if we take religious beliefs about afterlife seriously. Once again substantial, avoidable human suffering is a direct consequence of religious interference with our end-of-life decision-making. Udo Schüklenk

I told you I was sick.
Spike Milligan

3. Afterlife, immortality, heaven

✤ Do you want a life after death? Create a legacy worth remembering. When people speak of you, you will live again. Margaret Downey

> I'd like to go there (heaven). But if Jeffrey Archer is there, I want to go to Lewisham.
> *Spike Milligan*

✤ But all the works of human beings disappear and are forgotten in short order. ... even our cherished children and grandchildren ... our possessions will be dissipated ... our poems, books and paintings will be forgotten. Paul Kurtz

✤ 'The republic of heaven .... It stands for a sense of community. It stands for joy. It stands for a sense that the universe and we together, have a common meaning and a common destiny and a purpose. It stands for connectedness between these things. ... I don't want to be without heaven, but I can no longer believe in a Kingdom of Heaven. There must be a republic of heaven of which we are free and equal citizens – and it's our duty to promote and preserve it. Philip Pullman

✤ Belief in the afterlife does seem to take the 'sting' out of death for many older people with the hope of being re-united with loved ones. Peter Coleman

✤ The thought has surely occurred to many people throughout the ages: what if there is an afterlife but no god? What if there is a god but no afterlife. As far as I know, the clearest writer to give expression to this problem was Thomas Hobbes in his 1651 masterwork Leviathon. Christopher Hitchens

✤ The Good Guy's greatest joke is to make us believe in him, when he is not there at all, and his next best gag is the cruel lie about eternal re-union, about the Garden of Chums, the Bounteous Fellowship Cloister, Serenity Meadow, the Village with a Song in its Heart – he's had us all. Jonathan Meade

---

✤ To scientifically prove life after death is going to require carefully controlled experiments, not just a lot of stories. The plural of anecdote is not 'data'.

✤ Knowing that you are not going to live forever restores a true sense of your place in the scheme of things and you don't have to worry about hell; if you don't believe in the afterlife you will find more meaning and purpose in this world and live your life to the fullest since it is the only life you have.

✤ The hypothesis that those who believe in the afterlife will exhibit altruistic behaviour can easily be tested. We just need to gather a sample of those who don't believe in an afterlife and see whether they are significantly less virtuous than those who believe. *Victor Stenger*

- While religious people may look to a life hereafter, the only future life for humanists is that of future generations. Barbara Stoker

- Some theists believe in bodily resurrection. They are, of course, suitably baffled by the state and age of bodies so resurrected. The atoms constituting our bodies disperse over the years, even becoming a mish-mash of other humans. Peter Cave

- As a scientist, it's hard for me to regard immortality as a realistic prospect. I think conventional religion is a comfort to people. I think it fulfils a social and psychological function, and I don't want to belittle that. Joan Bakewell

- After the game the king and the pawn go into the same box. Italian proverb

- Good works, John Wesley insisted, are no guarantee of a place in heaven. But they are most likely to be performed by people who believe that heaven exists. Roy Hattersley

- If there is such a thing as re-incarnation, knowing my luck, I'll come back as me. Rodney Trotter

- I'd like to believe in heaven, not least because I'd like to meet my mum and dad again. I'd like to know if the welsh dresser was meant to go to me or my brother. John Peel

- **With a bit of luck your atoms may form a piece of lichen in the Lake District. Peter May**

- The belief in immortality should be exposed as a false hope. Death is final for everyone – the believer and the non-believer, the commander of armies and the lowly soldier, the dedicated teacher and the beginning student, the moral idealist and profligate hedonist. Nathan Bupp

- I do benefits for all religions. I'd hate to blow the hereafter on a technicality. Bob Hope

- When I approach the pearly gates, I'd like to hear a champagne cork popping, an orchestra tuning up, and the sound of my mother laughing. Patricia Routledge

- Your chilly sermons I can forego, this warm kind world is all I know. Willian Cory

- A peach-flavoured tea referred to 'Longevity Tea' is popular in many restaurants in the U.S. Olshansky and Carnes

- Old soccer players never die, they just achieve a final goal. Lewis Wolpert

- Where do all the football fans go? The great stadium in the sky? Anon

꙲ Never be a spectator to unfairness or stupidity. The grave will supply plenty of time for silence. Christopher Hitchens

꙲ He said his only remaining aims were 'to live until I am 90 and then to join my two wives'. Interviewee in Coleman study

꙲ Like all my fellow humans , I fear death, pain, loneliness, failure. It is painful to know that each of us is a finite being whose destiny is of no concern to anyone but those who love us. It is terrifying to realize that our unique individual knowledge will die with us and that even the memory of us will not last very long. Our sole traces will be our deeds in service of the human spark, guild marks on the bricks of a soaring Babel tower that constantly struggled to reach the stars. Athena Andreadis

---

꙲ I am in search of God. Can you direct me? 'Do not trouble about that,' said the young man, 'Take the world as it comes, for beyond it there is nothing. All roads end in the grave. *George Bernard Shaw*

꙲ Many god-believers who also believe in an afterlife inform me that, when I die, I will learn that they are correct. On the other hand, after they die, they will learn that I am correct, because I believe that after they die they will have no consciousness whatever (which would make it impossible to learn or experience anything). This is actually quite a fortunate circumstance, because for those who have given up many joyful experiences in this life. Who have sacrificed much for their god and his/her/its rules, it would be devastating to discover that there isn't an eternal reward for suffering through so much hardship.

꙲ Surely they surmise I must be devastated at the thought that when life ends, that's it. But I'm not, I wasn't upset throughout the infinity of time before I was born that I didn't exist. I won't lament not existing for the infinity of time after my death that I won't exist. I don't mind being unconscious under anesthesia when I undergo a surgical procedure. I have no problem with the non-dreaming parts of sleep. In short, if I had a choice, I would prefer a deep eternal sleep rather than an eternity of harp music. (No offence to my harpist friends)

Lori Lipman Brown

꙲ You might believe in an afterlife, but you're in no rush to perform the one experiment that could tell you if you are right. Leonard Mlodinow

4. Towards the end of life

❀ 'Home for Incurables' (Protestants), the 'Hospice for the Dying' (Roman Catholics) … grim names … in pre-war Liverpool. George Melly

❀ Sorrow binds people together, and assures the bereaved, that society shares and dilutes the pain. Even in a secular nation such sentiments are still a force for unity. Sorrow is a social adhesive. Steve Jones

❀ Old age would be the most happy of the stages of life, if only it was not the last. Countess Diane

❀ The leaves fall early this autumn, in wind … they hurt me. I grow older. Ezra Pound

❀ Many of us are too busy with the baggage of old age to waste time anticipating the finishing line. Penelope Lively

> ❀ Music is a medium in which to re-live and reconnect with past events and pleasures. It can 'bring both the dead and living to life'.
>
> ❀ There are a swirling mass of symptoms, sensations, emotions, impulses, thoughts, memories, perceptions, interactions, circumstances and situations at the end of life.
>
> Tia De Nora

5. Coming to terms with death

Those we love don't go away,
They walk beside us everyday
Unseen, unheard, but always near,
Still loved, still missed, and very dear

Poem for June Clarkson's funeral

☙ An individual human existence should be like a river – small at first, narrowly contained within its banks, and rushing past boulders and over waterfalls. Gradually the river grows wider, the banks recede, the waters flow more quietly, and in the end, without any visible break, they become merged in the sea, and painlessly lose their individual being. The man who, in old age, can see his life in this way, will not suffer the fear of death, since the things he cares for will continue. If, with the decay of vitality, weariness increases, the thought of rest will not be unwelcome. The wise man should wish to die whilst still at work, knowing that others will carry on what he can no longer do, and content in the thought that what was possible has been done. *Bertrand Russell*

Do not go gently into that good night
Old age should burn and rage at
The close of day
Rage, age at the dying of the light

Dylan Thomas

☙ Strong religious beliefs reduce fear of death, but 'confused' religious beliefs are not as powerful in so doing as compared to the 'non beliefs' of atheists and agnostics. Peter Coleman

☙ Death, in fact, helps living and the living. Without death, we may find it difficult to structure a life. With such immortality we should not recognize ourselves. Peter Cave

☙ To die completely, a person must not only forget but be forgotten. And he who is not forgotten is not dead. Samuel Butler

☙ Think of a hundred little memories you're glad to have had with your loved ones. Greg Epstein

☙ Instead of a constant struggle against death, life should be a never-ending search for new ways to appreciate each day that is lived. Lucretius

☙ The sudden awareness of our own finitude can surprise us into grief. There are words and places and snatches of music that overwhelm us with regret at the gliding away of the years and the remembrance of what has been taken away from us. Richard Holloway

🙏 Death affects us all. It is the most significant event of our lives. We are not around to worry about our forthcoming birth; we are around to fret over our inevitable death Peter Cave

🙏 I can't recall a specific conversation about the subject of death, but I know exactly what the response would have been: there is no afterlife; we are here and we are gone. Death is a fact; get used to it. And why are you just standing around with nothing to do. Barbara Ehrenreich

🙏 My husband keeps telling me that - unless you and I die, there will be standing room only, and shortly not even that on this planet. Margaret Bowker

🙏 Let us reflect on the human situation: all of our plans will fail in the long run, if not in the short. The homes we have built and lovingly furnished, the loves we have enjoyed, the careers we have dedicated ourselves to will disappear in time. The monuments we have erected to memorialize our aspirations and achievements, if we are fortunate may last a few hundred years.

🙏 We need to administer to the soul. As an alternative to the medicine men of the past, gurus, and spiritualists, soothsayers, rabbis, mullahs and priests, we need to demonstrate that life can be lived and live well without the illusions of religiosity.

Paul Kurtz

🙏 I do have empathy with those who wish to believe. I could have used some comfortable certainties when my father died. … And though Huxley and Hume and Epicurus have helped me, I do fear death, especially now that I've reached my father's last age. But I know that all the comforts and assurances I need, all we've ever really had, are those we get from those around us who have inherited the same strange scary wonderful conscious life that each of us has. *Dale McGovan*

🙏 It wasn't God, but music which consoled, and love and sympathy of others and support of a caring community. *Philip Kitcher*

❋ There is no cure for birth and death save to enjoy the interval. George Santayana

🙏 There was a long time when we were not; then there was a brief time when we were; and again there will be a long time when we no longer are. We are passing guests on earth, like the 60 billion human beings who preceded us.

But it is difficult not to be depressed by the prospect of leaving this earth. We feel just as we are getting the hang of the game and have wised up sufficiently to understand how to play it well, the whistle goes and the game ends. Marcus Brigstocke

6. Ceremonies, funerals, memorials

✣ As regards ceremonies, the greatest, most wide-ranging need among registered and unregistered humanists is the need for a humanist funeral ceremony. Levi Fragell

> ✣ A key experience in later life, with the capacity both to weaken as well as strengthen spiritual belief, is bereavement. Bereavements mount in number as people age.
>
> ✣ Humanist funerals can be extremely moving occasions because they are so personal. *Peter Coleman*

✣ I also show up at the funerals, memorial services or meetings of my near contemporaries. This is not so much for the sake of the departed, although if I have loved or admired them I'm glad to have the opportunity to stand up and be counted, but principally because those present tend to be old acquaintances too, whom I seldom or never see on other circumstances. Thus in cemetery, graveyard, chapel, public hall or public house, I find myself in touch with different segments of my diverse life: writers, painters, journalists or jazzbos, as the case may be. George Melly

✣ There was an uproar when Redditch Borough Council approved an ecologically, if not theologically sound plan to warm up the municipal baths with waste heated from a crematorium. (They went ahead anyway.) Steve Jones

✣ Memorial services are the cocktail parties of the geriatric set. Harold Macmillan

✣ They say lovely things about people at funerals. It's a shame I'm going to miss mine by just a few days. Bob Monkhouse

✣ In Norway young people from humanist families after receiving a course in moral studies, take part in a 'civil confirmation' ceremony in their humanist group, as a sign that they have become adult. Barbara Stoker

✣ Darwin doesn't provide much consolation at a funeral. Philip Kitcher

> ✣ *As much as I try to give religion and religious people the benefit of the doubt when possible, it is almost always a bad idea for a nonreligious family to stage a religious funeral for a nonreligious loved one who has died. At those moments when we are feeling most vulnerable, the last thing we need is false hope.*
>
> ✣ *The number of Americans who don't expect to have a religious funeral is in the stratosphere – nearly a quarter of us.* Greg Epstein

Secular funeral celebrants were specialists offering a range of 'customised, celebratory' funeral services' and presently conduct more than 60% of all funerals in New Zealand. They cater for the non-church-going lives and personalities of the deceased at the expense of religious interpretations of death. Celebrants come from a range of backgrounds – teaching, nursing and counselling. The majority were female. They described their services as 'personal', and created eulogies and tributes by family and friends of the deceased. They did more than collecting 'life-affirming laconic anecdotes' about the dead person. They commonly sought to draw out the 'essential' significance and meaning inherent in each life.

One funeral celebrant – Maria is quoted: 'Lots of people who led apparently unimportant lives, have actually been real characters. You've got to acknowledge the importance of their lives even if in the big scheme of things they're not seen as being very important.'

Celebrants also described the innate psychological need to acknowledge grief and elicit emotional expression. One celebrant stated – 'I think if no-one cries at a funeral, its not a good funeral.'

As far as bereaved people are concerned they had their own needs, preferences, and agendas. Sometimes there were thinly disguised tensions and conflicting demands in relation to the form of the funeral, even amongst family members. The expressed preferences – if any – of the dead person had to be reconciled with those of 'nearest and dearest' left behind.

Cyril Schafer

d) Non-belief, atheism, agnosticism, scepticism, science, free thought and secularism

1. Non-belief general

🐾 We have pushed ourselves out of the mainstream of human activities, through our endless discussions about religion and God: famously diagnosed as 'paralysis by analysis'. Babu Gogineni

🐾 We are supposed to think that a supreme being exists to follow the path of every particle while listening to every human thought, guiding his favourite football teams to victory, and assuring that the specially chosen survive plane crashes. Victor Stenger

🐾 I concluded at a very young age that God does not make things possible – hard work and determination do.
Margaret Downey

🐾 Isn't it enough to see a garden is beautiful without wanting to believe that there are fairies at the bottom of it too?
Douglas Adam

🐾 *I'm godless and content. I don't believe in unicorns, spaghetti monsters, giant mystical teapots orbiting the earth and I don't believe in God.*

🐾 *The map I had that used to tell me where to find him (God) turned out to be a blank sheet of paper with a question mark on it.*

🐾 *I don't believe in God but I hope someone somewhere continues to sing amazing songs to Him.*   Marcus Brigstocke

🐾 The great religions are the ships. The poets the lifeboats. Every sane person I know has jumped overboard. Hafiz

🐾 Most measures place the numbers of non religious at between 50% and 60% of the British population. Lois Lee

🐾 The air above Jerusalem is saturated with prayers and dreams. Like he air above industrial towns. Its hard to breathe.
Yehuda Amichai

🐾 You believe in God, and you think this is good and right. I don't believe in God and I think it is good and right.
Margarita Laski

77

🐾 When I go into prison as a prison visitor I have long chats with the prisoners … because most of them can't believe in God or don't believe in God. And if I challenge them about the fact that this is their only life and unless they correct it now they will never have another chance because there is nothing better waiting somewhere else, they do start to think about responsibility. … they do actually begin to think.

🐾 When I go into prison as a prison visitor I have long chats with the prisoners … because most of them can't believe in God or don't believe in God. And if I challenge them about the fact that this is their only life and unless they correct it now they will never have another chance because there is nothing better waiting somewhere else, they do start to think about responsibility. They do actually begin to think.

🐾 Now I can't do the loving God bit but I certainly think loving your neighbour is an important rule that we should all live by. I've had some neighbours I haven't liked very much but I think you never set out to deliberately harm somebody. *Minette Walters*

> 🐾 One good schoolmaster is of more use than a hundred priests. *Thomas Paine*

🐾 Blasphemy is a victimless crime. What do we call an ex-religious bloke? Godfrey. *Sikh website*

🐾 It is a failure of imagination not to see that when people go to art galleries, or concerts or enjoy gardening or country walks, or get together in the pub or around the dinner table with friends, that they are in different ways expressing themselves aesthetically and socially in the same (and arguably better) way as people who band together in congregations. AC Grayling

If you are not religious, for God's sake say so. BHA

If god did not exist, it would be necessary to invent him. Voltaire

How do you know you're God? Simple. When I pray to him, I find I'm talking to myself. Peter O'Toole

If there are no gods, then you will be gone, but will have lived a noble life that will live on in the memories of your loved ones. I am not afraid. Marcus Aurelius

> The north-south divide in the amount of non-religion matches the classical north-south defined by indicators of prosperity and deprivation: the line runs from the Severn to the Wash. The fault-line is likely to be economic in origin. A number of wards (population about 6000) are notably un-religious beyond the level expected. Several are found in towns such as Brighton, Bristol, Norwich and York, where urban liberals and the gay community appear to have a clear preference for living in particular distinctive neighbourhoods. *Voas &McAndrew*

🐦 It is not disbelief that is dangerous in our society: it is belief. George Bernard Shaw

🐦 I have no religious faith myself. I am an unbeliever but faith fascinates me. Matthew Parris

🐦 A group of Turkish businessmen once explained to me that the idea of human evolution was of course correct – except for the Turks, who had emerged from titanic figures that once roamed Anatolia. Steve Jones

🐦 Generally speaking, the errors in religion are dangerous, those in philosophy only ridiculous. David Hume

🐦 You can pray for someone even if you don't think the God exists. Gordon Atkinson

🐦 Since it is obviously inconceivable that all religions can be right, the most reasonable conclusion is that they are all wrong. Christopher Hitchens

🐦 I cannot believe in a God who has neither humour nor common sense. W Somerset Maugham

🐦 I prayed for freedom twenty years but received no answer until I prayed with my legs. Frederick Douglass

🐦 You can't convince a believer of anything; for their belief is not based on evidence, it's based on a deep-seated need to believe. Carl Sagan

🐦 God is a holding place for everything we don't understand. Betty Sue Flowers

🐦 The worst moment of my life as an atheist, was when my heart was overflowing with thankfulness and I had no-one to thank. GK Chesterton

🐦 I began to lose faith when I prayed to get into the school cricket team and had my prayer rejected. Sir Alfred Ayer

🐦 I believe in God, only I spell it Nature. Frank Lloyd Wright

🐦 If only God could make some clear sign! Like making a large deposit in my name at a Swiss bank. Woody Allen

🐦 I believe in sunshine, fresh air, friendship, calm sleep, beautiful thoughts. Elbert Hubbard

🐦 Out of all the people in these flats, there's only one person that I know that goes to church, funny isn't it? Interviewee in Coleman study

🐦 The term – 'non-religion' is not perfect: it is pragmatic. Lois Lee

🐦 Cupitt's prescription strikes us as rather like expecting people to continue to buy soccer tickets and gather in the stands to watch players who, for lack of a ball, just stand around. If there are no supernatural beings, then there are no miracles, there is no salvation, prayer is pointless, the Commandments are but ancient wisdom, and death is the end. In which case the rational person would have nothing to do with the church. Or, more accurately, a rational person would have nothing to do with a church like that. Daniel Dennett

> 🐦 I gradually came to distrust Christianity as a divine revelation.
>
> 🐦 The state of mind that grand scenes excited in me, can hardly be advanced as an argument for the existence of God.
> *Charles Darwin*

🐾 The flooding in Somerset is of 'biblical proportions' says an official. So it didn't happen then?

🐾 Praying I like a rocking chair. It gives you something to do, but won't get you anywhere. Gypsy Rose Lee

🐾 Blasphemy is a victimless crime.

🐾 I put monopoly money in the church collection plate. The vicar said – 'but that's not real money'. I replied – 'Well let's talk about this God of yours then!

🐾 I used to tell a lot of religious jokes – not any more. They put me on the sects' offenders register. *Joke website*

🐾 Life in any age is uncertain and indeterminate, fraught with tragedies: and so there is a deceptive quest for eternity, a search for moorings for our otherwise rudderless vessels in their uncharted seas of existence.

🐾 But if God is dead, what is the human prospect? Must it remain forever forlorn in a bleak universe? Is it possible to develop an authentic alternative that has some rational support? But to whom shall we turn for guidance? *Paul Kurtz*

🐾 The first stage of my disbelief came on at about 16, when the whole project began to look hopelessly implausible and more an invention to provide security and exercise social control through fear, authority and mystery. I could no longer believe that Jesus walked on water, or turned water into wine, or that there was a heaven and an afterlife. Such things seemed metaphysically inconsistent with that I knew of the world, and any scientific understanding of it. The whole thing seemed like a fairy-tale that had served a socially and psychological useful function in the past, but had just run out of gas. *Julian Sarulescu*

🐾 The world's great belief systems ... all require a leap of faith I am not willing to take. *Jack Dam*

🐾 Religion provides answers. You have a guardian angel; you saw Jesus; you went to heaven, you found your soul. These answers are false, but people are not going to give them up while they have nothing better to replace them with. *Susan Blackmore*

🐾 At last I was ready to admit to myself that I no longer believed in God. I'll never forget the sudden upsurge of relief when I finally acknowledged that my faith was gone. I felt suddenly free – free of the obligation to avow propositions I didn't understand, free of the struggle to make sense of doctrines that couldn't be made sensible and free of the need to square everything I learnt with the Catholic dogma. My only doxastic obligations henceforth would be to reason and evidence. 'Now', I thought to myself, all I have to believe is what I think is true'. *Louise Antony*

- What do people do when they discover that they no longer believe in God? Some of them don't do anything; They don't stop going to church, and they don't even tell their loved ones. They just quietly get on with their lives, living as morally (or immorally) as they did before. Anon

- The obvious conclusion is that our world would be better off if religion simply vanished from it. Philip Kitchner

- John Frazer, an Edinburgh apprentice, was charged with denying the existence of God, the devil, the immortality of the soul, and ridiculing the divine origin of the scriptures – saying 'they were only to frighten folk and keep them in order'. quoted by Ludovic Kennedy

- When asked whether they believed in God, most East Germans simply responded by saying – 'Nope, I'm perfectly normal'. Edgar Dahl

- There are several possible standards of proof – mathematical proof, proof beyond reasonable doubt, proof on the balance of probabilities and so on. I believe that the non-existence of God can be proved beyond all reasonable doubt. Nicholas Everitt

- The God I thought I believed in, was a very hard taskmaster, a cosmic big brother, endlessly looking down, marking my every fault, never satisfied with what I did. I was never able to please him, and indeed, never able to get in contact with him … when I eventually lost my belief in God, life became a whole lot better. Karen Armstrong

  - Rejection of faith has and will add to man's happiness and well-being. Charles Bradlaugh
  - I left the church the minute I left Ampleforth. Antony Gormly
  - There are a great many ways to 'not believe' and joining a group may be only one of them. Langston, Hammer and Cragun
  - Heresy is another word for freedom of thought. Graham Greene
  - When people cease to believe in God, they don't believe in nothing, they believe in anything. GK Chesterton
  - I don't believe in god, I believe in truth, I believe in human beings, I believe in justice. Natasha Kandic
  - In exchange for the security, comfort and certainty of the world's religions, we offer only doubts and uncertainty, a cold, hard, logical look at the universe. But I'll take it. Stewart Shapiro

🐾 I was not brought up with religious beliefs, because under Mao all religions were banned. Do I believe I God? No, but I do believe in some qualities – I would rank justice and kindness very high. Jung Chang

🐾 The sense of being well-dressed gives a feeling of inward tranquillity which religion is powerless to bestow. CF Forbes

🐾 My own spiritual leaning is towards the belief that God is the great outdoors. That the tide goes in and the tide goes out. Kate Clinton

🐾 I am not a religious person. My commandments are very simple: do not harm anybody or anything, whenever possible do good. Isabel Allende

🐾 A new term for us nonbelievers – 'Brights'. Daniel Dennett

> 🐾 People who don't believe - and many of my friends are non-believers. I certainly wouldn't like to lead that sort of life, in which they don't know where they are going. They can be kindly and so on, but it seems a life in which the light has gone out.
>
> 🐾 Clearly there are large numbers of non believers, every bit as virtuous as believers. *Gerald Priestland*

🐾 We should challenge the special authority that is accorded, all too often, to pontiffs, priests, and presbyters. This is a good time for atheists, sceptics, and rationalists, for humanists, doubters, … whatever we call ourselves- to stand up openly and start debating. There is no time like now to voice our disbelief. Russell Blackford

🐾 I certainly don't believe in a God who answers prayers, forgives sins, listens to misfortunes, cares about your sins, cares about your sex life, makes you survive death, performs miracles – that is most certainly a God I don't believe in. Einstein's God, which simply means the laws of nature which are so deeply mysterious that they inspire a feeling of reverence – I believe in that, but wouldn't call it God. Richard Dawkins

🐾 I just fell away from religion, in an exhausted and wearied way. Joan Bakewell

🐾 You won't burn in hell, but be nice anyway. Ricky Gervais

🐾 Darwin was a disillusioned theology student who harboured a bitter distrust of the Victorian God. He struck the decisive blow against that God. Deepak Chopra

2. Atheism

❧ We have tried out these ideas to propagate atheism in India. However gentle and benevolent our method was, 'atheism' as a philosophy had few takers during the 1980s. The word used here for an atheist is NASKIK, which literally means a non-believer, or a believer in nothingness. About 100 years back, to call someone an 'atheist' was tantamount to abuse. Even now, atheists are treated with suspicion, if not with total antagonism. *Sumitra Parmanabham*

❧ Atheism is a non prophet organisation.

❧ 17,000 atheists rioted this afternoon in the Middle East hours after a blank sheet of paper was found on a cartoonist's desk.

❧ An atheist walked into a bar with God, Odin and Zeus. The barman turned to him and said, 'Drinking alone again, I see.' *Joke website*

❧ There is now a large and growing literature — spanning dozens of books and hundreds of articles — attacking Richard Dawkins, Daniel Dennett, Christopher Hitchens and me (the so-called New Athiests) for our alleged incivility, bias and ignorance of how 'sophisticated believers' practice their faith. It is often said that we caricature religion, taking its most extreme forms to represent the whole. We do no such thing. We simply do what a paragon of sophisticated faith like Francis Collins does; we take the specific claims of religion seriously. *Sam Harris*

❧ It is difficult to be a good atheist … it is difficult to confront ambiguity, uncertainty, and the unavoidable losses of human life and choice, without clutching at false truths. Blackford and Schütclenk

God knows, I'm not the thing I should be,
Nor even the thing I could be
But twenty times I rather would be
An Atheist clean
Than under the gospel colours hid be
Just for screen

Robbie Burns

Here lies an atheist
All dressed up
And no place to go.

Epitaph

❧ Atheism is the true religion of peace. I have a nice peaceful lie-in every Sunday morning. Anon

❧ We're lucky to live in Berlin, a city where roughly two thirds of the population are atheists. Berlin atheist website

❧ I would argue that to be an atheist in Britain today is so mainstream that we can afford to become less strident in our criticism and more tolerant of those with a faith. Jim Al-Khalili

- My father was, and is, vociferously atheistic. If, as a boy growing up in York, I heard him answering a knock at the door with a brisk – 'bugger off', I knew it was the Jehovah's Witnesses who'd called. He listened to everything on Radio 4 except the Morning Service. As a boy I must have heard hundreds of times the continuity announcer saying : And now the Morning Service … today's broadcast comes from the church of …. Followed by the resonant click of the off switch. Andrew Martin

- The Godless of Gower Street. UCLU Young Atheists' Handbook

- I'm an atheist, and that's it. I believe there's nothing we can know except that we should be kind to one another and do what we can for other people. Katherine Hepburn

- Atheists (and agnostics) have a lower rate of divorce than some religious groups such as conservative protestant, largely due to difference in the age of marriage. Luke Gallen

- I have never been an Atheist in the sense of denying the existence of a God. I, for one, must be content to remain an agnostic. Charles Darwin

- The attitude of the globe's billion or to atheists to the doctrine of the devout majority … a mixture of fascination and distaste. Steve Jones

- As a 'cradle atheist' my attitude to religion has always been one of casual disinterest tinged with amusement and bemusement. Mitch Benn

- That's partly what I love about atheism: the quiet individualism, the self reliance, the lack of enforced singing, organised sanctimony, and bake sales. But then again, it can get lonely out there in splendid rational isolation. *Hermione Eyre*

- It wasn't easy being a child atheist during the Cold War. Barbara Ehrenreich

- I'm an atheist. There is a lot about the Catholic Church I don't approve of, simply because they don't approve of me. Ian McKellen

- Israel was created by people who didn't believe in God. Half the pioneers who built the country were hard core atheists. Uri Avneni

- Most atheists see little to be gained by broadcasting their beliefs. This defeatist attitude means that fundamentalists get away with spouting harmful nonsense. Nathan Bupp

---

- Although atheism might have been logically tenable before Darwin, Darwin made it possible to be an intellectually fulfilled atheist.
- We are all atheists about most of the gods that humanity has ever believed in. Some of us just go one god further. *Richard Dawkins*

> ❋ Can atheists claim on insurance for an 'Act of God'?
> ❋ Atheism - putting the logical into theological. *Sikh Website*

❋ What makes me an atheist? ... If what you hold sacred is not any kind of Person you could pray to, or to be an appropriate recipient of gratitude (or anger, when a loved one is senselessly killed), you're an atheist in my book. If, for reasons of loyalty to tradition, diplomacy, or self-protective camouflage (very important today, especially for politicians), you want to deny what you are, then that's your business, but don't kid yourself. Maybe in the future, if more of us 'brights' will just come forward and calmly announce that of course we no longer believe in any of those gods, it will be possible to elect an atheist to some office higher than a senator. We now have Jewish and female senators and homosexual members of Congress, so the future looks bright. Daniel Dennett

❋ I am a Church of England Atheist. Philip Pullman

❋ While having a Phd is no guarantee of atheism or secularity, a strong relationship between them exists. Coleman, Hood and Snook

❋ I admire the 'new atheists' because they seek to right the very real and very many religious wrongs of our time. Greg Epstein

❋ Endorsement of a secular scientific world view can provide secular benefits ... for a non believer that a religious world view has for believers. Studies of atheists have indicated they derive happiness and fulfilment from their affinity for logic and science. Luke Gallen

❋ The lack of atheist converts is only natural, after all people who aren't Manchester United fans don't feel the need to join the Not the Manchester United club. Alan Marshall

❋ I fear that I have become only an impure atheist. After all I enjoy English parish churches, with their simple pieties, their quiet graveyards, remembering past generations ... the overwhelming sadness of lives cut short by ... outsider's wars, pestilence, accidents. I slip furtive coins or small notes into the preservation fund. It is hard to confess, I can enjoy religious music. I suppose I regard the Church of England as an old family pet: a bit moth-eaten, prone to scratch its own fleas (gay marriage and female bishops), but familiar and somehow comforting. Simon Blackburn

❋ Atheists refuse to believe in the 'old man in the sky'. Hector Hawton

❋ Did you hear the news? 230 girls kidnapped by Atheists in North Sweden in ongoing fighting with Agnostics in the south of Sweden. Sik'pedia website

❋ Most of the people I know at university are cheerful atheists. Daniel Garber

❋ An atheist is a man who has no visible means of support. John Buchan

I am an atheist … Well I think I am; or was. I might be a lapsed atheist, having a crisis of whatever the opposite of faith is – facts? I'm having a crisis of facts. My atheism is quite wobbly at present. I haven't watched a David Attenborough documentary for months and I don't have a pop science book on the go. Forgive me secularism, for I have sinned.

Even the most devout atheists continue to put their praise and reverence somewhere.

Atheism is well represented amongst comedians, though it's important to recognize that atheist comics find they get more comedy mileage out of discussing their rejectionist position than the believer comic does from discussing theirs.

Atheism is no more a badge of being clever than going to Oxford for a day trip and coming back with a special hat that says 'I went 2 Oxford' on it.

I am an atheist by default. I am a moderately well read atheist, but one without a sense of my secularism serving any real purpose. It's not proactive or positive. I don't feel any better about being an atheist than I do about wearing glasses.

I would rather be happy than right. I know that some atheists are so happy that they are right that the two things mean exactly the same thing.

Marcus Brigstocke

When we have eaten a strong-tasting dish in a restaurant, we are often offered a sorbet to cleanse our palate so that we can taste the next course properly. An intelligent atheist critique could help us to rinse our minds of the more facile theology that is impeding our understanding of the divine.

These 'new atheists' one has to choose between science and faith, and religion is the cause of all problems of our world! It is the source of absolute evil and 'poisons everything. They see themselves in the vanguard of a scientific/rational movement that will eventually expunge the idea of God from human consciousness.

The new atheists show a disturbing lack of understanding or concern about the complexity and ambiguity of modern experience, and their polemic entirely fails to mention the concern for justice and compassion that, despite their undeniable failings, has been espoused by all three of the monotheisms.

These new atheists show little concern about the poverty, injustice and humiliation that has inspired many of the atrocities they deplore; they show no yearning for a better world. They do not appear to consider the effect of such nihilism on people who do not have privileged lives and absorbing work. It is difficult to see how theologians could dialogue fruitfully with Dawkins, Harris and Hitchens, because their theology is so rudimentary.

Karen Armstrong

✤ I think we are in grave danger from atheism and idolatry in their various forms - whether the worship of the state, the class, the party, pleasure, possessions, or power. Gerald Priestland

✤ When I was a very small human, an over-enthusiastic public school scripture teacher told our class that children who didn't believe in God got leprosy. When I got older and realised atheism didn't need to carry a gangrenous health warning. Emma Tom

✤ There is truth in Marx's dictum that religion is the opium of the people, but the consumption should be seen as medical rather than recreational. The most ardent apostles of science and reason recommend immediate withdrawal of the drug – but they do not acknowledge the pain that would be left unpaliated, pain too intense for their stark atheism to be a viable solution. Genuine medicine is needed, and the proper treatment consists of showing how lives matter. Philip Kitcher

✤ I'm a hardcore atheist - I don't believe people believe in God. Sikh website

✤ Militant atheists should accept that this is a Christian country.
Eric Pulling, then Master of Faith

✤ I'm a casual atheist - I don't follow religiously. Wikipedia website

> ✤ The best way to become an atheist is to read the bible from cover to cover.
>
> ✤ Scientists have to stop sitting back and start stepping up to challenge religion. The welfare, and indeed the survival, of our species is at stake.
> *Victor Stenger*

3. Agnoticism

I peered into ... Loch Ness ... you never know. But then in matters of the Loch Ness monster I am not a disbeliever, rather a Nessie agnostic. Blackford and Schüklenk

David Hume, TH Huxley, Robert Ingersoll all knew that God does not exist, but they never said so. They said they were sceptics or agnostics. Philip Kitcher

I am an agnostic who relishes the equipment of Christianity: its mythology, its buildings, its ceremonies, its music, the whole edifice. Penelope Lively

4. Scepticism

❦ Secularism has two primary meanings: the first asserts the freedom from government imposing a religion or set of beliefs upon people. The state is neutral on the matter of belief and gives no privileges or subsidies to religions. In its second sense it argues that activities and decisions, especially political ones, should be based on reasoning and evidence and not religious influences. Phil Wood and Charles Landry

❦ A new term for a secularist - an 'AWEIST' who has a profound feeling of wonder at the world. Philip Zuckerman

❦ Secular identity is multi-dimensional, multi-faceted, nuanced and diverse - no more or less than religious identity. Langton, Hammer and Craigen

❦ All communist states established in Eastern Europe after the Second World War followed the example of the USSR in attempting to impose secular alternatives to religion. However, the results achieved varied from country to country. Peter Coleman

❦ **Men occasionally stumble over the truth, but most of them pick themselves up and hurry off as if nothing has happened.** Winston Churchill

> ❦ *Dawkins' website is a hub for the lonely secularist seeking the spiritless joy of communion and mutual approval of other non-believers.*
>
> ❦ *But believer, atheist, agnostic, or other, it would be particularly depressing to be run over by the big secular bus, wouldn't it?*

❦ Conflicts having a primarily doctrinal basis tended to last ... secular wars, in contrast, continue on average for less than half a decade. Steve Jones

❦ Denmark is a healthy, happy, contented, law abiding and good society. As far as mortality is concerned many Danes see death as the end. They live the one life they have fully. And the reason for this Danish utopia? The more secure a society and the more egalitarian, the less religious it need be. If one self and one's children can lead a happy prosperous life, free of war and fear of crime, if there is good health care, why be concerned about afterlife? Insecurity generates both widespread death anxiety and widespread need for religious consolation. Phil Zuckerman

❦ A far safer route to national cohesion is secular schooling. A C Grayling

❦ Some of the most secular countries, such as those in Scandinavia, are among the least violent, best educated, and most likely to care for the poor. Greg Epstein

❦ Secular - from the Latin *saicularius* meaning worldly. Jonathan de Jong

❦ It's been said that the secular world art fills a God-shaped hole ... the Tate Modern as a modern cathedral ... these are places for pilgrimage. They create moments where people have a sense that the world is larger and more confusing than they thought. Karen Armstrong

❦ That young people are more likely to find ecstasy in a dance hall than in a church or invest energy and wealth in a football team than worshipping God seems pretty compelling evidence for the secularisation paradigm. Steve Bruce

❧ *For the secular community to come together and press for rationalism, knowledge, learning, science and reason to be held up as the holiest of holies is something I support wholeheartedly.*

❧ *Every group claims to be under-represented; secularists really are.*

❧ *Secularists have as much right to be heard as anyone else, even if as a group their opinions are disparate. I believe that a common goal amongst secularists is to push for humanity as we experience it here and now to be respected, before we consider how to please something that no-one can prove is waiting for us when we're finished living.*   Marcus Brigstocke

Secularism has its own revered figures, people who met personal tragedies without turning to illusionary comforts. Hume faced his painful death stoically, persisting in his scepticism to the end. TH Huxley, Darwin's tireless champion wracked with grief at the death of his four-year-old son, refused Charles Kingsley's offered hope of a re-union in the here-after.

Hume's and Huxley's heirs, like Richard Dawkins, for example, preach eloquently to the choir, but thoughtful religious people will find their bracing message harsh and insensitive. How can these celebrants of secularism what many other people stand to lose if their arguments are correct? How can they expect people to be grateful for the mess of pottage they offer?

Some secularists can find the resultant picture of the world, and our place in it, unbearable. William James' arresting image of the high cliffs that surround a frozen lake, on which the ice is slowly melting, testifies to his own yearnings for some way of enlarging, or enriching the scientific world-view he felt compelled to accept.   *Philip Kitcher*

"What a way to go."   RMB

5. Science

🔥 Today the scientific investigation of miracles, stigmata relics and shrouds provides naturalistic explanations. Agree with Daniel Dennett that we need to press into service our knowledge of the brain, and consciousness, biology, and genetics. Also social sciences to provide … explanations for the persistence of religious beliefs and practices. Paul Kurtz

> Science is not just another kind of religion … a pernicious view. The difference is that science works.
>
> *Richard Dawkins*

> Human beings have only 23,000 genes, of which 65% are so basic that we share them with a banana. Deepak Chopra

🔥 Our secular and scientific culture has not replaced or even challenged these mutually incompatible, supernatural thought systems. Scientific method, scepticism or rationality in general, has yet to find an overarching narrative of sufficient power, simplicity, and widespread appeal to compete with the old stories that give meaning to people's lives. Ian McEwan quoted by Jerry Coyne

🔥 The one thing you must beware of is the so called 'God of the gaps', the idea that because scientists at this particular time can't explain this or that phenomenon then we must wheel in a god to plug the gap. That's been the way it's worked for hundreds of years and of course God has got successively squeezed out of the gaps until he's more or less pushed right back to the beginning of the universe to the Big Bang itself and that's the only place that you need this poor old God. Paul Davies

🔥 Declining religious belief has relatively little to do with an increase in the scientific mindset advocated by atheists such as Dawkins. Indeed an emphasis on scientific and rationalistic thinking as well as on religious belief appears more common in older than younger people. Coleman

---

🔥 Science shows that many of our perceptions lie between the ears as much as the world outside or, for that matter, beyond … Neuroscientists have scanned the brains of devout subjects as they think elevated thoughts … they have found separate areas that light up when a subject experiences an intimate relationship with the deity (right), fear of his power (left) and doubts about his existence.

🔥 When religious shackles are at last struck from their wrists, men and women, wherever they are, will no longer depend on the dubious promise of a serpent. Instead they will be free to form a single community united by an objective and unambiguous culture whose logic, language and practices are permanent and universal, it is called science.

Steve Jones

🔔 The often – heard statement that religion and science are compatible is a mere chimera, a frail argument that is easily demolished. Consider: religion offers no evidence, no proof, no testable statements, as part of its claim. In fact I'm constantly faced by the smug statement that 'God doesn't need to be proven,' and to the religious that's that. Science on the other hand, demands evidence, proof, testable statements. These two approaches to reality are totally incompatible, in absolute opposition, and one of them derives from wishful thinking. I'll let my reader decide which one that is. James Roni

🔔 As an adult, surrounded by science and reason, it's obvious that God doesn't exists. Zoe Margolis

🔔 One's convictions should be proportional to one's evidence. Sam Harris

🔔 Science flies you to the moon. Religion into skyscrapers.

Joke Website

🔔 Unlike religious people, who may make some of their decisions according to what the Bible says (or the Qur'an, or other sacred writings) or what their church teaches, humanists can only rely, in the last resort, on their own judgement based on probabilities indicated by the scientific method. Barbara Stoker

---

🔔 Science is not the lord of modern life, it is the under-appreciated servant.

🔔 With the exception of a handful of creationists, motivated by their religious beliefs, no scientist doubts the basic idea of Darwinian evolution, or that natural selection is the mechanism behind it.

🔔 Scientists employ precise objective measurements and precise objective concepts for good reason, and the fact that they seek to ensure that their measurements and concepts are not influenced by 'love, trust, faith, beauty, awe, wonder, compassion etc, does not mean that they dismiss the value of these qualities in other areas of life.   *Leonard Mlodinow*

🔔 The idea of an inherent conflict between religion and science was and is false. They are of equal worth for human life and remain logically distinct and fully separate in lines of enquiry.

Scientific rationality can tell us why we have cancer; it can even cure us of our disease. But it cannot assuage the terror, disappointment and sorrow that come with the diagnosis, nor can it help us to die well. That is not within its remit.

Karen Armstrong

🝆 Compassion, awe, devotion, and feelings of oneness are surely among the most valuable experiences a person can have. What is irrational and irresponsible in a scientist and educator, is to make unjustified and unjustifiable claims about the structure of the universe, about the divine origin of certain books and about the future of humanity on the basis of such experiences.

The Templeton Foundation, an organisation that claims to seek answers to 'life's biggest questions,' but appears primarily dedicated to erasing the boundary between religion and science. Because of its astonishing wealth, Templeton seems able to engage the complicity of otherwise secular academics as it seeks to rebrand religious faith as a legitimate arm of science. *Sam Harris*

🝆 To understand the story of evolution - both its narrative and its mechanism - modern Darwins don't have to guess. They consult genetic scripture.

Matt Ridley

🝆 Most claims about God are completely untestable, but those that can be tested, like the power of prayer or the existence of miracles, fail the tests.

🝆 Yet this negative evidence rarely convinces everyone. Anecdotes from friends, TV shows about faith healing, and the results from poorly designed studies that seem to show miraculous effects all have far more power over people than the best scientific evidence seems to do.
Susan Blackmore

6. Free thought

⚜ Free thought … the lovely term that first appeared in England in the late 17th century and was meant to convey devotion to a way of looking at the world based on observation, rather than on the ancient 'sacred' writings by men who believed that the sun revolved around the earth. Susan Jacoby

⚜ Freethinker – one who doubts or denies religious dogma. Corliss Lamont

⚜ Freethinkers naturally mistrust uniforms. We don't want to conform to wearing our hair in a certain way or adopting a vestigial hat. We have no symbolic trinkets, no karas or rosaries; no arcane taboos, no dietary requirements, no cult pronouncements … Better surely to express your atheism through a thousand rational acts; through constant low-level vigilance, through countless tiny words and deeds. Hermione Eyre

❦ *Responses to statements such as 'I am certain god exists', 'I pray everyday', 'my holy book is true', 'Mine is the one true religion' can sort out the sanctified sheep from the sceptical goats.*

❦ *Arguments about the merits or otherwise of belief (let alone of particular faiths) tend to degenerate into slanging matches, with each side picking facts to fit its case, although it must be said that at least in the modern world the facts seem increasingly to support the sceptics.*
                                                                Steve Jones

❦ I believe that our obligation is to make life better because it's our obligation to each other as human beings, not in relation to eternal rewards and infernal punishments. Susan Jacoby

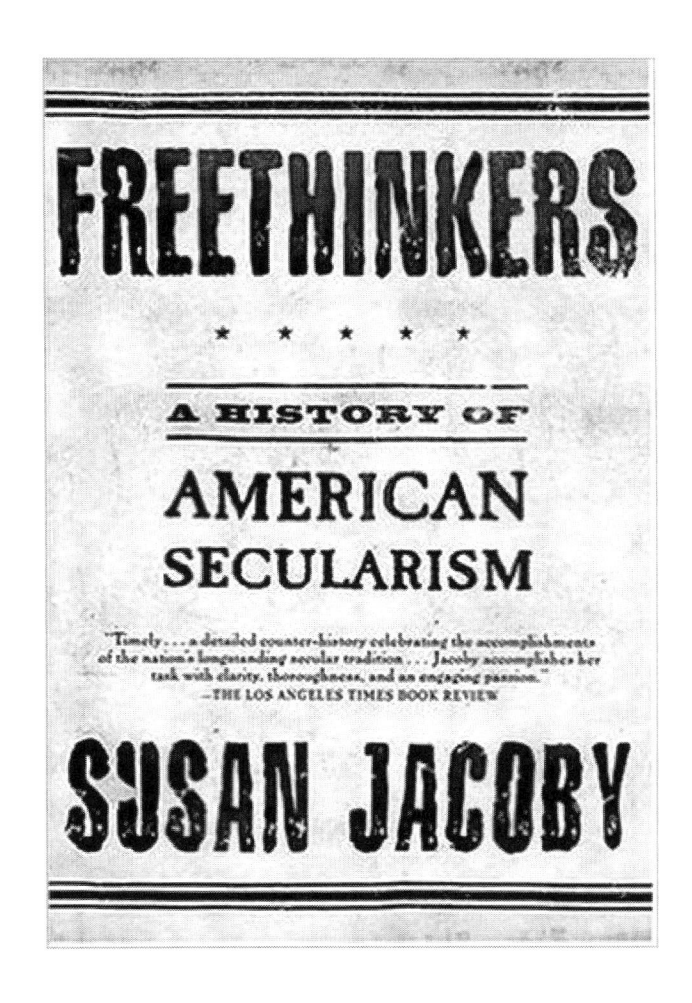

7. Securalism

🙰 Secularism is usually about as popular as taxes. With the exception of France, one would be hard-pressed to find a country on earth where a large number of citizens get enthusiastic about secularism.

🙰 Secularism is not in any way opposed to religion. Rather it does not approve of certain types of relations between religion and government…. It ensures that, as bearers of faith or no faith, they are all equal before the law.

🙰 Secularism's defenders are stationed in print and television newsrooms. They worked in cinema and the domain of high art. Down on the campus there were entire platoons of bespectacled secularists who sympathized with the cause.

🙰 Millions and millions of people are already living secular lives. They are believers and non-believers, Protestants and Muslims. The goal should be helping people, as they are and where they are, to recognize that they already abide by core secular and secularish virtues.

🙰 The secularish are the types of people who have no difficulty in missing daily prayers. A secularish Jew can miss lots—conceivably a lifetime of Sabbath services, as a secularish Catholic might avoid Mass. A secularish Muslim might enjoy a good strong drink every day after work. Coffee might be the jump-start to a secularish Mormon's morning routine.

🙰 A new vision for secular America, wherein both freedom of and from religion are granted as much space as possible. Jacques Berlinerblau

🙰 The actual number of seculars in the world i s actually quite small outside of Europe and Manhattan. Rick Warren

🙰 It is fair to say that God has had a hefty advantage over the secular for a very long time. John Humphreys

> **Lighthouses are more helpful than churches.**
> Anon

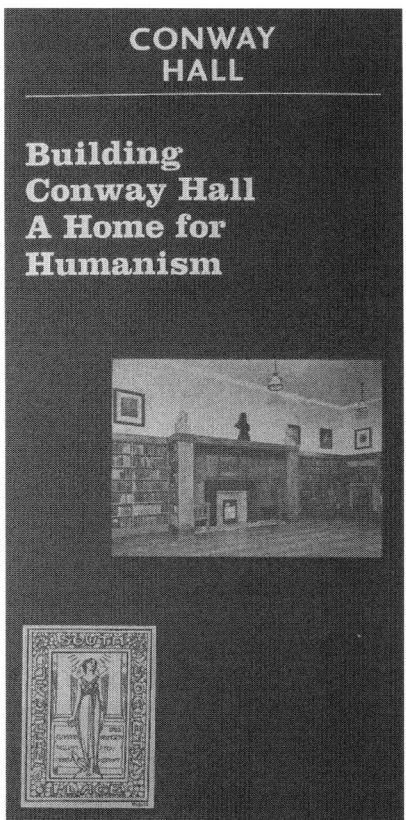

The faces and places of humanism

CHAPTER 4
HURRAH FOR HUMANISM

1. Definitions of humanism

✤ Those who follow superstitions or horoscopes or who say prayers or believe in a future life cannot be humanists. Barbara Stoker

✤ Defining humanism … live life, love other people and leave the world a better place. Anon

✤ Understanding the world without God, giving sense to the world without God, is the heart of today's humanism. There are two segments here; understanding how things are; understanding how things ought to be. Peter Cave

✤ To the question – 'What do I want?' The humanist replies: why not happiness and a full life?' To, 'How can I face death?' He responds – 'Why not with resolute courage?' And to –'How shall I live fully?' He responds – 'By sharing the creative joys and sorrows of life with others'. Nathan Bupp

✤ For the humanist, the mourning process begins with accepting that death is real and final and that, with apologies to Epicurus, we fear it. Greg Epstein

✤ Humanism is a general outlook based on two premises. The first that there are no supernatural entities or agencies in the universe, the second that our individual ethics must be drawn from, and responsive to, the facts about the nature and circumstances of human beings. AC Grayling

✤ The only difference between a religious humanist and a secular humanist is what they do on a Sunday. Fred Edwards

✤ Humanism is not a dogma or creed, and there is a wide diversity of humanist viewpoints. It expresses the belief that man has potentially the intelligence, good will and cooperative skills to survive on this planet, that there is a good life to be had 'on this side of the grave', and, however short may be one's days, beauty and joy may fill them. Edwin Wilson

✤ Happiness, health, freedom, tolerance and love are keywords in the humanist vocabulary. They indicate the general direction in which we are determined to move. They are like points of the compass rather than a detailed map. Hector Hawton

✤ Secular humanism as we know it today, is mostly associated with the humanist philosopher Paul Kurtz. This unbelievably prolific University of Buffalo professor, (an entire book is needed to catalogue all of his writings) set up his offices in Amherst, New York, in the sixties. Jacques Berlinerblau

✤ Actually what I would really like to do is to get up on the topmost tower of the mosque, grab the microphone and perform an alternative humanist call to prayer. 'Good morning everyone. Have you considered doing a decent thing for another human being today? Not for an eternal reward but just because people are fundamentally worthwhile.

✤ You have to be careful with the word humanist. Especially when you say it out loud. If you don't watch yourself it can sound awfully similar to humourless, and they're anything but that. *Marcus Brigstocke*

✤ Humanism holds that the race of man is the present culmination of a time-defying evolutionary process on this planet that has lasted billions of years ... that after death there can be no personal immortality ... humanism gives special emphasis to man's appreciation of the beauty and splendour of nature ... humanism is international in spirit and scope ....

✤ The main thrust of humanism is not simply to espouse the negative – what we do not believe in – but what we do. We should not begin with atheism or anti-supernaturalism but with humanism. I am a secular humanist because I am not religious. I draw my inspiration not from religion or spirituality but from science, ethics, philosophy, and the arts. I call it eupraxsophy. This term is derived from Greek roots and literally means 'good practice and wisdom'. It is a secular outlook which provide illumination, meaning and direction to the art of living.

✤ The humanist is open to the subtle nuances of human experience, but he insists that we use our powers of critical judgement to appraise the claims to truth. Although our fondest hopes and desires may demand life before birth or after death, the evidence points in the other direction. *Paul Kurtz*

✤ Humanism is not a religion. Humanism has no popes or perfect people. Humanists accept that the scientific evidence for evolution is overwhelming and build our world view around it. The real point of humanism is that God is beside the point.

✤ Humanism is goodness without god. It is about engaging with life, acknowledging the reality of ageing, sickness, death, and other problems, so that we can learn to most fully appreciate the time, health and life we have.

✤ The responsibility for our lives and the kind of world in which we live is ours and ours alone. *Humanist Manifesto*

We need more books like this   *Conway Hall - a Cathedral of Secularism*

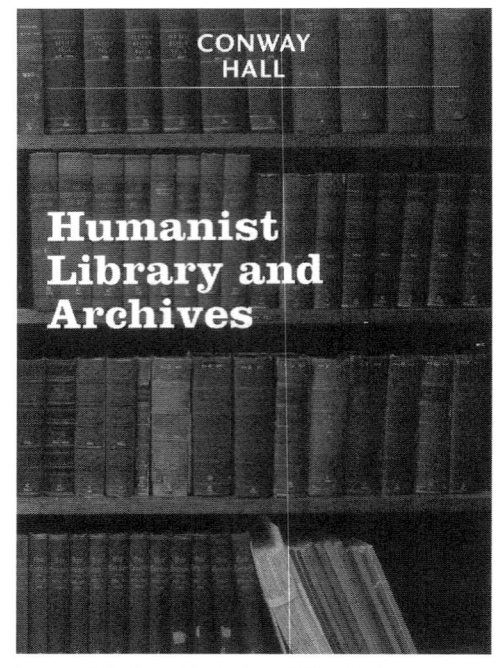

2. What is humanism?

- Why did we come together to edit a volume of humanist thought? Why did we ask some 50 scientist, philosophers, science fiction writers, political activists, and public intellectuals from across the globe to put down in writing the reasons that convinced them personally that there is not an all-powerful, all knowing, good and loving God watching over us? Blacker and Schüklenk

> There is no humanist answer book, but there are definitely humanist values. Henry Hawton

- Reason, rationality and reasonableness have been use to describe the methodology that humanists have advocated.

- Originally humanism was a revolutionary weapon in the hands of free thinkers who demanded freedom from authoritarian ecclesiastical control. Subsequently, humanism was refined and expanded to express a this-worldly concern for human happiness and for a humane and just society. *Paul Kurtz*

- The first principle of humanism is a commitment to free enquiry in every field of human endeavour. Nathan Bupp

- Atheistic humanism has four leading characteristics – curiosity, a free mind, belief in good taste, and a belief in the human race. EM Forster

❧ Humanism is a general outlook based on two allied premises ... there are no supernatural entities or agencies in the universe. Our individual and social ethics must be drawn ... from human beings. AC Grayling

❧ The humanist virtues are: a regard for what is true, personal responsibility, tolerance, consideration, breadth of sympathy, public spirit, co-operative endeavour and a concern for the future. Barbara Stoker

❧ What we offer here, then, are not manifestos or creeds. We want to simply explain what we believe, and why we believe. That in the end, is the best we can do. *Louise Anthony*

> ❧ Being good defines me as human. Anyone who wants to be good because they think they should be, not because their religion tells them to be, to me is a humanist.
>
> ❧ I am well aware that some other atheists would call me an accommodationist. However this patronising term needs to be replaced, so I have thought long and hard in search for an alternative – a more appropriate one to define my brand of atheism – until I realised it has been under my nose all the time: it is being called a humanist. *Jim Al-Khalili*

> ❧ Some felt they had no need of a religious belief and were untroubled by this absence of belief. 'I had a long life sustained by the arts – music and visual arts ... I do believe that people are disillusioned with their beliefs in old age because they have had naïve beliefs in the beginning. I think it is probably my stance as a humanist paradoxically makes me interested in people's attitude to religion. I feel it so peripheral to real life yet so many people seem unable to envisage being without what I consider to be 'fairy tales'. Interviewee in Coleman study

2a) What is not humanism?

❧ Humanists encourage us to make the best of our lives, lives containing meaning and purpose, without resorting to superstition and the supernatural.

❧ Humanists often think – aspire, hope, trust – that, once that they have exposed religions absurdities, life's puzzles may be ironed out at least a little, that cooperation, reason, and empathy may come to the rescue ... over how our lives may be improved and how to view meaning and death. Peter Cave

❦ The terms 'humanism' and 'religion' should have clear definitions so that the temptation to describe the former as a species of the latter can be scrupulously avoided. Some succumb to this badly mistaken temptation because they wish humanism would be a movement with a credo that would sustain the formation of communities of like-minded folk, who hold mutually supportive meetings and the like – making it a substitute for membership of a congregation of the faithful in one or another faith. But humanism is no such thing, and religion is quite a different thing.

❦ Religious folk try to turn the table on people of humanistic outlook by charging them with 'faith' in science or faith in reason. Faith, they seem to have forgotten, is what you have in the face of fact and reason. Science is always open to challenge and refutation, faith is not. By definition, in short, humanism is not religion, any more than religion is or can be a form of humanism. *AC Grayling*

❦ Humanism cannot in any fair sense of the word apply to one who still believes in God as the source and creator of the universe. It surely does not apply to God-intoxicated believers. Paul Kurtz

3. What humanists believe

> For humanists, earthly life is all we have.
> *Peter Cave*

❦ There is no evidence of an eternal state of existence or of a blessed union with God. The evidence for survival is based on wishful thinking and is totally inconclusive. Death seems to be the natural state of all life forms, even though modern medical science and technology are able to ward off disease and prolong life. Humanism is thus sceptical about the entire drama of the theistic universe: that God exists and that we can achieve salvation in an afterlife.

❦ Here is the humanist life stance: humanists do not look upward to a heaven for a promise of divine deliverance. They have their feet planted squarely on Mother Earth, yet they have the promethean fortitude to employ art, science, sympathy, reason, and education to create a better world for themselves and their fellow human beings.

❦ Secular humanists are dismayed by the tenacity with which believers cling to their hopes of life eternal. Why are so many people deluded by a false promise of after life? Such individuals lack the courage to become what they wish. They lack the audacity to create their own world of hopes. They overlook the fact that life can be intrinsically worthwhile for its own sake; it can overflow with exciting expectations and anticipations. Our hopes are as unlimited as our reams of a better tomorrow.

Paul Kurtz

- Humanism is one of the most influential and yet most maligned philosophies of all time. Unfortunately most people don't know anything about it. To make matters worse, there are a lot of people who are already humanists and just don't know it. Jen Hancock

- The confident secular humanist view proposes a set of civic values and rules of engagement, which include providing settings for a continually renewing dialogue across differences, cultures and conflicts; allowing strongly held beliefs or faiths expression within this core agreement; acknowledges the 'naturalness' of conflict and establishing means and mediation devices to deal with differences. It seeks to consolidate different ways of living, recognising arenas in which we must all live together and those where we can live apart. Phil Wood and Charles Landry

- When humanists are referred to disparagingly as 'unbelievers' it is conveniently overlooked that they have a much richer and more extensive set of beliefs than those they abandoned. Henry Hawton

- Humanism's answer is: so long as we continue to grow in some way, we are living, not dying. Greg Epstein

- It would be nice if some of the people who stopped believing in God started to believe in humanism. Laurie Taylor

- Watching my son laugh as he rides a bike for the first time. Taking my daughters … skiing for the first time in two feet of virgin powder snow. Paddling out in the surf in the early morning sun … as the first wave hits me in the face. That is what I believe in now. Julian Savulescu

---

I am a humanist, which means in part, that I have tried to behave decently without any expectation of rewards or punishment when I'm dead. Kurt Vonnegut

---

- Humanists lack scriptures, revelations, and miracles; it lacks bishops, rabbis, and imams. Humanists do not burn books, threaten eternal damnation, or take offence at anti-humanist cartoons.

- We humanists have only stories, plays and music to represent lives, to inspire us. *Peter Cave*

- My own intellectual life began the moment I ceased to believe in God. Thought is essentially curious and sceptical. It is interested not in the question, 'How wonderful are things as they are?' but in the question, 'Why are they as they are and might they be better?' John Harris

The humanist should not be fearful of being labelled: that is a trap for the timid. One can, I submit, be a liberal humanist, a Marxist humanist, a radical humanist, a conservative humanist, even a reactionary humanist.

Humanists disagree about many things in the political and social sphere. Humanism is not a dogmatic creed. Humanists share with orthodox Christians and Jews any number of social ideals. Humanism does not have a doctrinaire political platform on which it stands. Any effort to politicize humanism in a narrow sectarian way is unfortunate. Paul Kurtz

How can humanism be a guide to the perplexed unless it offers plain, unambiguous advice? In fact, the critics continue there is no such thing as humanism. It is just a patchwork made of bits and pieces taken from the history of philosophy.

In Marxist jargon humanism is a 'bourgeois ideology'. Humanists have no such massive organisation like the church, and as individuals some are socialists and some are not, but all are democrats in the ordinary usage of that much abused word. There is no humanist answer book, but there are definitely humanist values. Henry Hawton

4. Humanist Ceremonies

- Performing wedding ceremonies for humanist couples deeply committed to a long-term, exclusive life partnership is one of my favourite parts of my job as a humanist chaplain. Greg Epstein

- There is rising secularism in UK funeral practice. This in terms of both software and hardware. Anything may be provided from a humanist ceremony, via a 'pick 'n mix', through to 'full on religion'. Mortuary Journal.

- (Religious) rituals are an important part of everyday life – they are a way to honour, remember, mark milestones, rejoice, grieve, instil a sense of belonging and place But many rituals are secular. Even handshakes demonstrate feelings of warmth and respect for those we meet. Should we have humanist rituals equivalent to crossing oneself? Or always wear the humanist badge? And what about life cycle ceremonies and festivals – secular celebrations of humanity, friendship, kinship, neighbouring, intergenerational solidarity, nature, beauty, art, music, love, giving, sharing, singing, eating and drinking? Scott Lowe

- A humanist funeral is one when people organising the funeral run it without mentioning a God or afterlife. Shapi Khorsandi

- Each year the number of humanist ceremonies goes up. Yet they are still pitifully few. James Meek

5. Humanist institutions

※ There is no humanist party line. Paul Kurtz

※ First, an observation. Go out in the street and ask a stranger – any stranger will do – 'Have you heard of any of these organisations: the IRA, Al-Qaeda, and last but not least, the International Humanist and Ethical Union (IHEU)?' I guarantee you that the vast majority will have heard of the first two, but will be nowhere near the foggiest with the last. To my mind this is a tragedy. Shirley Dent

> ※ *For the active minority, the British Humanist Association lectures, campaigns and meetings supply a sense of community among the godless.*
> Hermione Eyre

※ Many of our (humanist) associations do not offer members any specific advantages or 'benefits'. The annual membership fee thus becomes a diffusely grounded moral obligation, while a number of other organisations deal more effectively and discernibly with the individual issues that together form the basis for the humanist platform – from euthanasia to human rights. Levi Fragell

6. What humanism means for living

※ Humanism isn't concerned with talking the good talk. You actually have to walk the good walk to be considered an ethical person. If you fail, we won't tell you that you are going to Hell. We will simply choose to avoid you in future. Anon

※ One complaint often heard against humanism is that it is too vague and amorphous and that it does not apply its ideal principles to practice. *Nathan Bupp*

※ Many (Thames Path humanists) just lead their lives as non believers. M. Eglelke

※ Telling people that I am a humanist has led to many wonderful conversations with complete strangers about the positive attributes of our philosophy. I have had such conversations in supermarkets, fast food restaurants, bars, and children's play groups. Jennifer Hancock

※ And don't forget the many thousands of secular humanists who have given their lives for Democracy, or Justice, or just plain Truth. There are many ideas to die for. Daniel Dennett

※ We should treat others as we would like to be treated ourselves. Humanist Society, Scotland

※ One of the biggest challenges to humanism is the need to transform itself from an academic world view to a practical way of life. It is high time that humanists concentrated on the real issues that confront the majority of people. Poverty, inequality, injustice, oppression, social justice and equity are the issues that matter to the poor and downtrodden. How to inculcate the scientific temper among ordinary people is another major challenge. Vikas Gora

❧ This apparently trivial fetish (about the pig) shows how religion and faith and superstition distort your whole picture of the world. The pig is so close to us, and has been so handy to us in many respects, that a strong case is now made by humanists that it should not be factory-farmed, confined, separated from its young, and forced to live in its own ordure.
Christopher Hitchens

❧ Humanism is deeply concerned with the responsibility of each succeeding generation to bequeath to the future a world as good to live in as possible. After all, while religious people may look to life hereafter, the only future life for humanists is that of future generations. Barbara Stoker

❧ The good life is one inspired by love and guided by reason.
Bertrand Russell

❧ Humanism combats the despotism of religion, but why not the despotism of the market?
Babu Gogineni

❧ The neutral state, the secular state, advocated by humanists is not an atheist state.

❧ As for the electorate being well informed, much information is by way of slick advertisements determined by political wealth, and crude misleading headlines encouraged by a few non-elected powerful editors. Humanists, naturally, are much concerned by all this. Humanists aspire to a level playing field.

❧ Although the big dilemmas of death and life impress our thoughts, we frequently manifest who we are by the small and seemingly significant Little everyday courtesies, kindness and thoughtfulness —they matter too. Humanists, dare I say, when on trains, would not rest their dirty shoes on seats opposite.

❧ Humanists do not shield their eyes from life's woes, tragedies and sheer horrors often deliberately inflicted by man. Humanists can be angry at humanity's inhumanity.
Peter Cave

❧ The theatre and ritual of religion – the Mass, communal prayer, weddings, funerals and the like – answer a need many people have for communal celebrations of significant moments in life and death. Humanist groups can offer non- religious versions of some of these observances for those who do not construct their own way of joining with friends and family to effect them. It is a failure of imagination NOT to see that when people go to art galleries or concerts or enjoy gardening or country walks, or get together in the pub or round the dinner table with friends, that they are in different ways expressing themselves aesthetically and socially in the same (and arguably better) way as people who band together in congregations. *AC Grayling*

Daniel Dennett describing his thoughts on surviving a life threatening condition and having come through a major operation ...

> ❋ In Kansas City, Missouri, a local humanist group hosted poetry reading, jazz and blues performances, soul food dinners and other cultural activities of interest to many African Americans.
> *Norm Allen*

Yes I did have an epiphany. I saw with greater clarity than ever before in my life that when I say Thank Goodness, this is not merely a euphemism for Thank God. We atheists don't believe that there is any God to thank. I really do mean thank goodness. There is a lot of goodness in this world, and more goodness everyday, and this human-made fabric of excellence is genuinely responsible for the fact that I am alive today. It is worthy of the gratitude I feel today, and I want to celebrate the fact here and now.

To whom, then, do I owe a debt of gratitude? To the cardiologist who has kept me alive and ticking for years and who swiftly and confidently rejected the original diagnosis of nothing worse than pneumonia. To the surgeons, neurologists, anesthesoilogists, and perfusionist who kept my system going for many hours under daunting circumstances. To the dozen or so physician assistants, and to nurses and physical therapists and X-ray technicians and the small army of phlebotomists so deft that you hardly know they are drawing your blood, and the people who brought the meals, kept my room clean, did the mountains of laundry generated by such a messy case, wheel-chaired me to X-ray and so forth. These people came from Uganda, Kenya, Liberia, Haiti, the Philippines, Croatia, Russia, China, Korea, India – and the United States, of course – and I have never seen more impressive mutual respect, as they helped each other out and checked each other's work

But for all their teamwork, this local gang could not have done their jobs without the huge background of contributions from others ... Allan Cormack who shared the Nobel prize for his invention of the CT scanner ... I am also grateful to ... Science, Nature, Journal of the American Medical Association, Lancet, and all the other institutions of science and medicine that keep churning out improvements, detecting and correcting flaws.

Do I worship modern medicine? Is science my religion? Not at all; there is no aspect of modern medicine or science that I would exempt from the cost rigorous scrutiny, and I can readily identify a host of serious problems that still need to be fixed .... Had I had my blasted aorta a decade ago there would have been no prayer of saving me.

The best thing about saying thank goodness in place of thank God is that there really are lots of ways your debt to goodness – by setting out to create more of it, for the benefit of those to come. Goodness comes in many forms, not just in medicine and science. Thank goodness for ... music, for fresh drinking water on tap, for food on our tables. Thank goodness for fair elections and truthful journalism. If you want to express your gratitude to goodness, you can plant a tree, feed an orphan, buy books for schoolgirls in the Islamic world, or contribute in thousands of other ways to the manifest improvement of life on this planet now and in the near future.

❧ This conclusion, that this is the only life I get, makes every moment extremely precious. I relish the experiences I enjoy in this life. I recognize and thrill to the fact that my body feels healthy and I am able to be active. I lament the times when ill-health, weather, other people's behaviours, or random chance make my days more difficult. I strive to make the world better for future generations in the light of the fact that I believe they too will only get one chance to enjoy the world during one lifetime each. I work to help those who need a hand because I do not believe that a supernatural outside force can be relied on to do so. It is devastating to discover that there isn't an eternal reward for suffering through so much hard-ship.
Lori Lipman Brown

❧ Human beings are so constituted that periodically they seek out 'ekstasis', a 'stepping outside' of the norm. Today, people who no longer find it in a religious setting, resort to other outlets: music, dance, art, sex, drugs or sport. We make a point of seeking out these experiences that touch us deeply within and lift us momentarily beyond ourselves. At such times, we feel we inhabit our humanity more fully than usual and experience an enhancement of being. Karen Armstrong

❧ Today's humanism is, then, atheism-agnosticism plus, the plus being the belief in shared human values and rationality. Peter Cave

---

Humanism as Activity

❧ *Humanism is a philosophy which must be defined by action as well as logic and words. Hence humanism is: a man and woman standing in awe of the aurora borealis or with creative delight in the glow of having made a cake, a chair or a garden.*

❧ *A woman labouring with strength and dignity to deliver a child.*

❧ *A gentle touch on a mourning shoulder upon the death of a friend or relative.*

❧ *An attitude of openness towards persons of other cultures, races, clans and viewpoint; an eager willingness to engage in dialogue towards other humans.*

❧ *An enthusiasm for getting up in the morning to see what one can learn from other humans.*

❧ *A sense of wonder in staring upwards at the Empire State Building or Michaelangelo's Dome on St Peter's or Mt Fujiama or staring downward at an iceberg from a jet off the coast of Greenland.*

❧ *The deep satisfaction of hearing a simple, Well Done from a respected person, solution of a complex problem, the climbing of a mountain, the identification with a team which has won a hard game or even lost it with dignity.*

❧ *Tears while watching a friend die from cancer.*

❧ *The humanist-in-action will need to recognize the need for humour.* Roy Fairfield

❋ There is a growing awareness that deeds can be more important than creeds, acts more important than words.

❋ Common Moral Decencies – (i) Integrity: truthfulness, promise keeping, sincerity, honesty. (2) Trustworthiness: fidelity and dependability. (3) Benevolence: good will, …. (4) Fairness: gratitude, accountability, justice, tolerance, and cooperation.

❋ Thus there is a basic principle of motivation that the sceptical humanist insists upon: that life is good, or can be good, and that living is better than dying. Indeed, it can be exciting, full of joy and zest.

> To the question:
> 'What do I want?'
> the humanist replies,
> 'why not happiness and a full life'?
>
> To:
> 'How can I face death?'
> he answers,
> 'Why not with resolute courage?'
>
> And to:
> 'How shall I live fully?'
> he responds,
> 'By sharing the creative joys and sorrows of life with others'.

❋ Despite the current downturn, the modern global economy is still productive beyond the wildest dreams of earlier civilizations, offering consumers a staggering range of products and services. So many conveniences and inventions are available to make life a source of comfort and enjoyment … there are so many exciting activities and hobbies to captivate our interests … concerts, politics, books and films, art galleries, antiques, growing lovely gardens in the back of the house, visiting far off places, raising funds for worthwhile causes, enjoying love and sex, our families and grandchildren growing up, taking exercise. In other words, the list of things to do today is virtually endless, depending on the culture in which we live.

Paul Kurtz

7. Opposition to religion(s)

❋ Replacing religion with reason alone creates problems if we neglect and allow to wither an open and political public domain. Reason then becomes the domain of the lawyer and the bureaucrat who hand down their judgements to a disengaged public as prescriptively as a priest or imam. Phil Wood and Charles Landry

❋ When humanists become vocal about the dangers of religion, they are not making a big fuss about kindly and tolerant Church of England vicars who share tea and cucumber sandwiches with parishioners.

❋ But whatever humanists do, whatever tangles we live, whatever stances we adopt – whatever slight angles we take on the universe – we know they are our own. There is no-one out there, in a heaven or hell, to whom to pass the buck. Peter Cave

❋ For many of us, the humanist stance is a very lonely one. Humanists are people that generally go against the stream, placing doubts on what others accept as absolute truths. Living among religious people, or in a religious environment is quite a normal situation and one that generally doesn't worry us. Secular institutions enrich our lives through the diversity they preserve and promote … attacking religiously biased public institutions is a task we have never evaded. Hugo Estrella

❋ It would be nice if some people who stopped believing in God started to believe in humanism. The late Linda Smith to Laurie Taylor

❋ Unlike Christians, humanists see no virtue in faith, blind obedience, meekness, unworldliness, chastity, or pointless self denial. Barbara Stoker

❋ To create alternatives to religion, new programmes and agendas or cultivate enquiry and human enrichment, focussing on the meaning of life and providing passionate-rational guides, instead of cathedrals, temples and mosques that have dominated the cultural landscape for so long. Paul Kurtz

❋ Dawkins, Hitchins and Harris are 'fundamentalists', immoderate, hard-line, with simplistic views of theology and presenting religion at its absolute worst. Karen Armstrong

❋ Of course secular humanists see 'spiritual religion' as a last desperate attempt to claim a privilege for traditions whose credentials have been decisively refuted. They point to non religious literature which can equally move and inspire. And the unquestionably secular elements to be found in religious practices. Humanists enthusiastically endorse compassion and social justice so what more has spiritual religion to offer over and above this. The answer lies in its social function, which is 'unlikely to disappear without a struggle'. Philip Kitcher

8. Diversity

- Humanists are just a bunch of individuals in a stew of rationality. Joke website
- On the difficulty in organising humanists … it's like herding cats. Humanists are fiercely individualistic people. Stephanie Kirmer

> Humanists recognize that humans form a motley crew; and a motley crew they should remain.
> *Peter Cave*

- The humanist should not be fearful of being labelled: that is a trap for the timid. One can, I submit, be a liberal humanist, a marxist humanist, a radical humanist, a conservative humanist, even a reactionary humanist.

- Humanists disagree about many things in the political and social sphere. Humanism is not a dogmatic creed. Humanists share with orthodox Christians and Jews any number of social ideals. Humanism does not have a doctrinaire political platform on which it stands. Any effort to politicize humanism in a narrow sectarian way is unfortunate. *Paul Kurtz*

- How can humanism be a guide to the perplexed unless it offers plain, unambiguous advice? In fact, the critics continue to state there is no such thing as humanism. It is just a patchwork made of bits and pieces taken from the history of philosophy.

- In Marxist jargon humanism is a 'bourgeois ideology'. Humanists have no such massive organisation like the church, and as individuals some are socialists and some are not, but all are democrats in the ordinary usage of that much abused word.

- There is no humanist answer book, but there are definitely humanist values. Henry Hawton

9. Future of humanism

❦ Western arrogance and biased Eurocentric thinking have been obstacles to developing humanism worldwide. Today there are groups in Ghana, Nigeria, Tanzania, Ethiopia, Uganda and other nations. Indeed the potential for spreading humanist ideals far and wide in Africa is immense. Norm Allen

❦ Why is humanism not the pre-eminent belief of humankind? Joyce Carol Oates

❦ What will it take for a new humanism to arise? One that is diverse, inclusive, inspiring, and a transformative force in the world today. Greg Epstein

❦ The future of secular humanism … 'I gotta wear shades'. Davis Silverman

Music is the future of humanism

Gilad Atzman

"The way to go!"

CHAPTER 5
KEY STATS AND MAPS

Here some handy statistical and cartographic information is presented to show some of the major trends and patterns in terms of religion and 'non religion' in the UK and in the world.

Most data is gleaned from official sources in the UK – Office of National Statistics and the 2001 and 2011 censuses. There are alternatives and a lot depends on what precise questions are asked. The question – what is your religion? was the only 'voluntary' one. In the 2011 census 7.2% of people did not answer the question. Is it about affiliation, belief, belonging and practice?

In the US in 1990 the ARIS survey asked 'What is your religion?'. In 2001 the question was amended: 'What is your religion, if any?' Victor Stenger argues for more nuance in the questions asked – not forgetting the 'Don't Know' option and five-point likert scale to draw out what respondents actually believe. Bias in survey research is not unknown and statistics can, of course, be highly contested. Maps can have a propagandist flavour.

First, let's have some key statistics of a 'macro' nature.

United Kingdom

- There are 10 million people aged 65 and over living in the UK; Over 14million aged 60 and over and this figure will rise to 20 million by 2051
- 6% of Britons regularly attend a religious service
- The Church of England has 15,700 church buildings. 57% in rural areas where only 17% of the population live
- Fifty years ago over 50% of the population of the UK went to church on a weekly basis. Today only about 15% attend church on a monthly basis
- 93% of those claiming 'No religion' in England and Wales in 2011 were born inside the UK
- In the British Social Attitudes survey the number of people over the age of 60 reporting to be Christians decreased from 74% to 66% whereas those reporting no religion increased from 20% to 29% over the period 1991-1998
- In 2001 7.7 millions stated they had 'no religion' in England and Wales. In 2011 it was 14.1 millions (round a quarter of the population. *ONS Dec. 2012*
- There was an increase in those reporting 'No religion' between the 2001 and 2011 censuses from 14.8 to 25.1%
- 800 Church of England parishes have ten or fewer adults in regular attendance
- In 2011 in the UK 1,285,489 older people (60 and above) stated they were of 'no religion'; (794,187 males and 491,302 females)
- In the UK, a 2006 poll by the BBC asked 2,000 people to describe their view of

how life formed and developed. While 48% accepted the evolutionary view, 39% opted for creationism or intelligent design, and 13%didn't know

- There remains a significant proportion of the population of the UK – much greater than those who attend football games, for example – for whom the church remains a part of their lives
- A poll in 2009 found that 84% of Christians thought that religious freedom of speech and action was at risk in the UK

2. Europe

- A third of Czechs belief in the afterlife
- In the Netherlands affiliation to Christian churches dropped from 76% of the population in 1958 to 40% in 1999
- Belief in a personal God remained strongest in Eastern Europe (>80%), and in Greece, Cyprus, and also Portugal
- Eurobarometer found that in 2005, on average 52% of people in the 25 countries in the EU at that time, stated that religion was an important part of their lives. In the UK it was 45%, Romania 8% and Bulgaria 42%

3. North America

- In 2007 the Pew Research Centre found that the US scored 1.5 on a scale measuring religiosity, compared to a range from 0.25-0.75 in Western Europe
- The proportion of Americans who actually belong to a specific church congregation (as opposed to naming a religious preference when asked) has hovered around 65% for many decades
- 20% of Americans describe themselves as evangelical Christians (45m in total)
- According to ARIS (American Religious Identification survey) in 2001 the three categories with the largest gain in membership were evangelical /born again (42%), non denominational (37%) and no religion (23%)
- In the US, of those born in 1945 or before – 70% believed in the existence of God and prayed daily, those born after this date 53% believed in the existence of God and 41% prayed daily
- Less than half of those aged 85 years and older in San Francisco stated that religion was important in their lives
- One in four young adults say they have no religion, and will not have a religious funeral. However, half of all Americans say they would not vote for a well-qualified atheist candidate for public office. 49% of American Jews say they are not Jewish by religion
- Some 3,500 to 4,000 churches are closed in the US annually
- America's religious geography has been transformed since 1990. Religion-switching, together with Hispanic immigration, has changed the religious profile of some states and regions. The proportion of Catholics has increased to 37% in California and 32% in Texas
- Only 9-14% of Americans believe that evolution is NOT God-guided. (About the same percentage of Americans who do not belong to any church

- *Michael Shermer in the 'Science of Good and Evil', (quoted by Stenger) cites a survey in 1950 in which atheists and agnostics were more willing to help the poor than those who rated themselves as 'deeply religious'; a 1975 study which showed that college-age students in religious schools were no less likely to cheat than their atheist and agnostic counterparts in non-religious schools; a survey of studies in the psychology of religion revealed a consistent positive correlation between religious affiliation, church attendance and so on with ethnocentricism, authoritarianism, dogmatism, intolerance of ambiguity, and specific forms of prejudice, especially against Jews and blacks*
- A 1998 study (also cited by Stenger) found that only 7% of the members of the American National Academy of Sciences believed in a personal God. Another study conducted amongst scientists from 21 top American universities found that 31% were atheists, 31% were agnostics, 15% believed but had doubts, 10% were sure there was a God, and 5% believed in God 'sometimes'. Disbelief was greatest amongst physicists and biologists, each with about 70% atheists or agnostics, and only 6-7% 'true believers'
- 47% of Americans surveyed by the University of Minnesota said they would 'disapprove' if their child wanted to marry an atheist
- 27% of all Americans do not expect a religious funeral at their death

4. World wide

- There are over a billion 'non religious' people around the world
- James A Haught (quoted by Victor Stenger) presents a range of statistical evidence that religion is waning in advanced nations – In France fewer than 7% of adults regularly worship. In Denmark and Sweden fewer than 5% of adults are in church on a typical Sunday; the Archbishop of Dublin graduated only one priest in 2004; In Britain only 4% of children attend Sunday school compared to 50% in 1900; the Anglican church in Canada lost more than half its members between 1961 and 2001; in Japan 77% of adults say they do not believe in a specific religion, although many practise a uniquely Japanese form of spirituality.
- Women outnumber men by a ratio of 3:2 in most Christian churches in the west
- There are more than 1bn Muslims in the world, in over 57 different nations
- Belief in life after death is a widespread notion, but not unanimous; perhaps 1-2 billion living people don't believe in it
- The Catholic church has 1.1bn members worldwide
- There are 1.3bn Muslims in the world today. Only 7% of Muslims interviewed in 35 countries said that they believed that the 9/11 attacks were justified
- Current estimates place the number of the non religious in the world at 26% excluding China (44% including China)
- In 1993, there were in the region of 12.8m Jews worldwide
- There were 300,000 Christians missionaries worldwide, 69,000 from the USA (1993)
- Countries in which humanism is strongest include Norway, Netherlands, UK, Germany, Canada and India

Integrated household survey (April 2010 to March 2011)

Question: What is your religion, even if you are not currently practising? (Soliciting information about religious affiliation and identification with a religion irrespective of actual belief and practice).

Answer: Nationally (GB) 69% Christian, 4% Muslim and 23% No religion.

Response by age group

	Christian	No religion
< 16 years of age	69.7	29.0
16 – 24 years	58.9	31.6
25 – 34 years	66.4	34.5
35 – 49 years	66.8	25.0
50 – 64 years	78.3	15.9
> 65	87.6	8.4

20 most 'No religion' local authorities in England and Wales (2011 ONS census)

1. Norwich	2. Brighton and Hove
3. Blaenau Gwent	4. Caerphilly
5. Rhondda Cynon Taff	6. Cambridge
7. Bristol	8. Bridgend
9. Hastings	10. Torfaen
11. Merthyr Tydfil	12. Portsmouth
13. Ipswich	14. Nottingham
15. Hull	16. Exeter
17. City of London	18. Stevenage
19 Swansea	20. Harlow

David Voas and colleagues have analysed the pattern of belief/disbelief in Britain in a series of scholarly articles. They point out that gender (females more religious than males), family background (for children with Christian parents there is a 88% chance they will be so; if they have non religious parents between 4% and 5% chance, education (graduates are more secular), place of residence are all factors in explaining why some people are 'religious' and others are not as already noted.

Geographically there is 'an unbuckled' British bible belt in the north west and north east of England, as seen above local secular micro climates in cities like Brighton, Norwich, Nottingham and Bristol. Why should this pattern exist? The answer lies in such factors as the legacy of Irish immigration in Lancashire, and newer migrants in London who fill evangelical churches, as opposed to the concentration of students, young and well paid service workers in southern towns and cities.

Finally, since older people tend to be more religious than younger, the age profile of places is significant. Today's elderly population have not become more religious as they have aged, they were more likely to have gone to Sunday school. Tomorrow's seniors are likely to be unbelievers – thus a 'cohort' rather than an 'age' factor at work in explaining changing patterns of identity/belief/behaviour.

No religion by age 2011 (England and Wales

Age group	% people
0-24	39%
25-49	42%
50-64	13%
65+	6%

Total % by age category
The number and percentage of all age categories stating that they had 'No Religion' increased in all age categories between 2001 and 2011, with lowest increase being recorded amongst older people.

North of the border
The Scottish census asked: What religion, religious denomination, or body do you belong to? A different, but arguably just as leading a question, as in England and Wales. Despite this a total of 1,921,018 people ticked the 'No religion' box. And a total of 1,941,000 a non religious one – that is a 37% increase since the last census.

Aberdeen (48%), Fife (46%), and Edinburgh city/ Midlothian and the Shetland Isles (45%) recorded the highest 'No religion' rates. 366,039 did not complete this voluntary question. 2,992 wrote that they were humanists, 2,848 Atheists, 1,818 Agnostics, 37 free thinkers, and 18 secularists.

Atheism in America and the Arab world

10 'Scariest' states in USA to be an atheist			
1	Louisiana	6	North Carolina
2	Mississippi	7	Alabama
3	Rhode Island	8	Arkansas
4	Texas	9	Idaho
5	Florida	10	Pennsylvania
(Waleed Al-Husseini)			

Number of atheists in Arab Countries			
Egypt	866	Jordan	170
Morocco	325	Sudan	70
Tunisia	320	Syria	56
Iraq	242	Libya	34
Saudi Arabia	178	Yemen	2

Total 2,293 non believers out of a population of over 300 million.
(Egyptian Islamic Institute)

KEY STATS AND MAPS

Religious affiliation, English regions and Wales, 2011

Percentage of Population

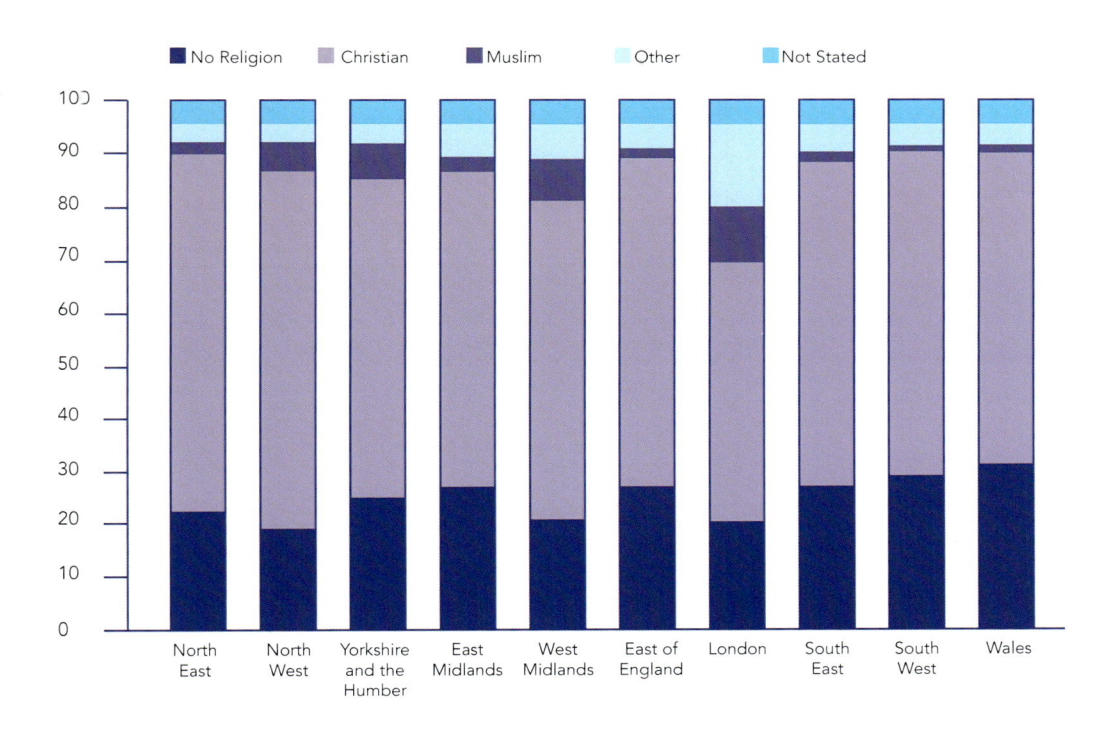

In comparison with 2001:

- The proportion reporting no religion increased across all regions - ranging from 5.0 percentage points in London to 13.6 percentage points in Wales

- Christian affiliation fell across all regions - ranging from 9.8 percentage points in London to 14.3 percentage points in Wales

- London had the largest increase of Muslims (3.9 percentage points) and Hindus (1.0 percentage point)

- Within the other religious groups, the largest increase of Sikhs was in the West Midlands (0.4 percentage points)

Differences in religious affiliation across local authorities

Christians formed the majority religion across most areas in England and Wales. In over nine in ten areas, the proportion of people who were Christian was over 45 per cent. It was the largest religion in all local authorities except Tower Hamlets where there were more people who identified as Muslim.

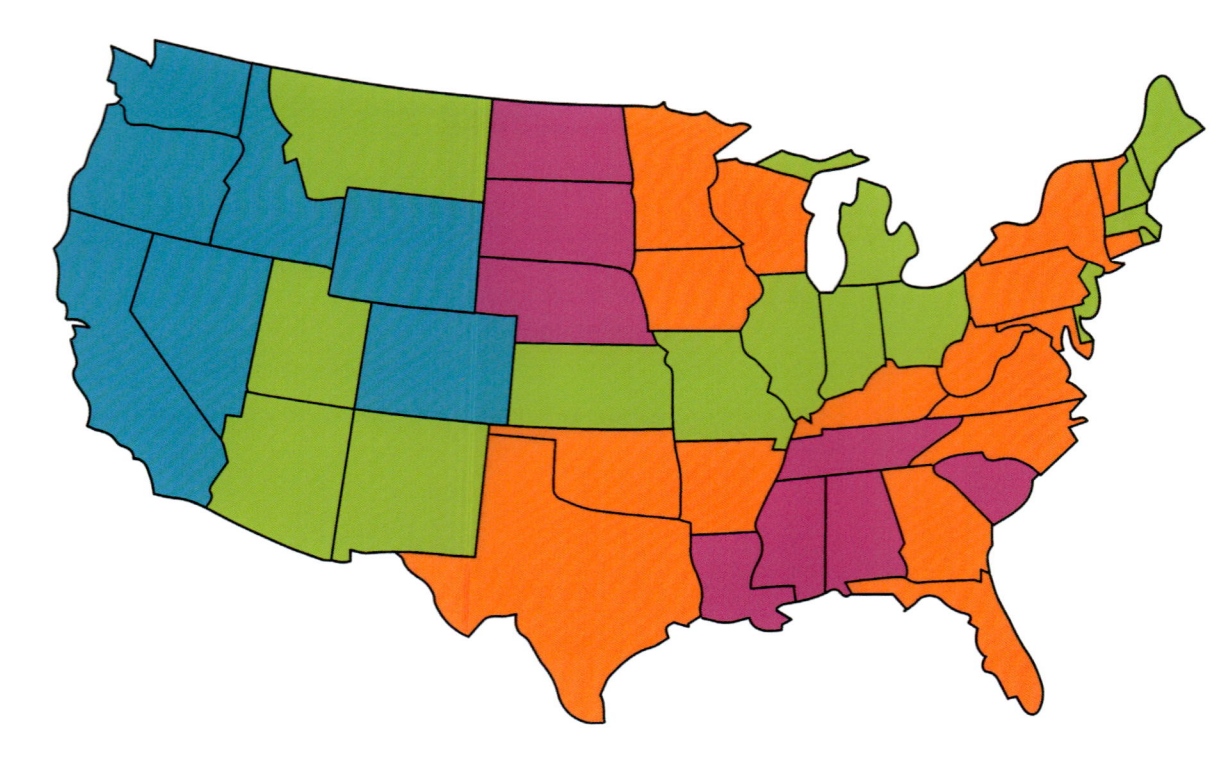

Map of the US showing the percentage of people who did not claim religious affiliation

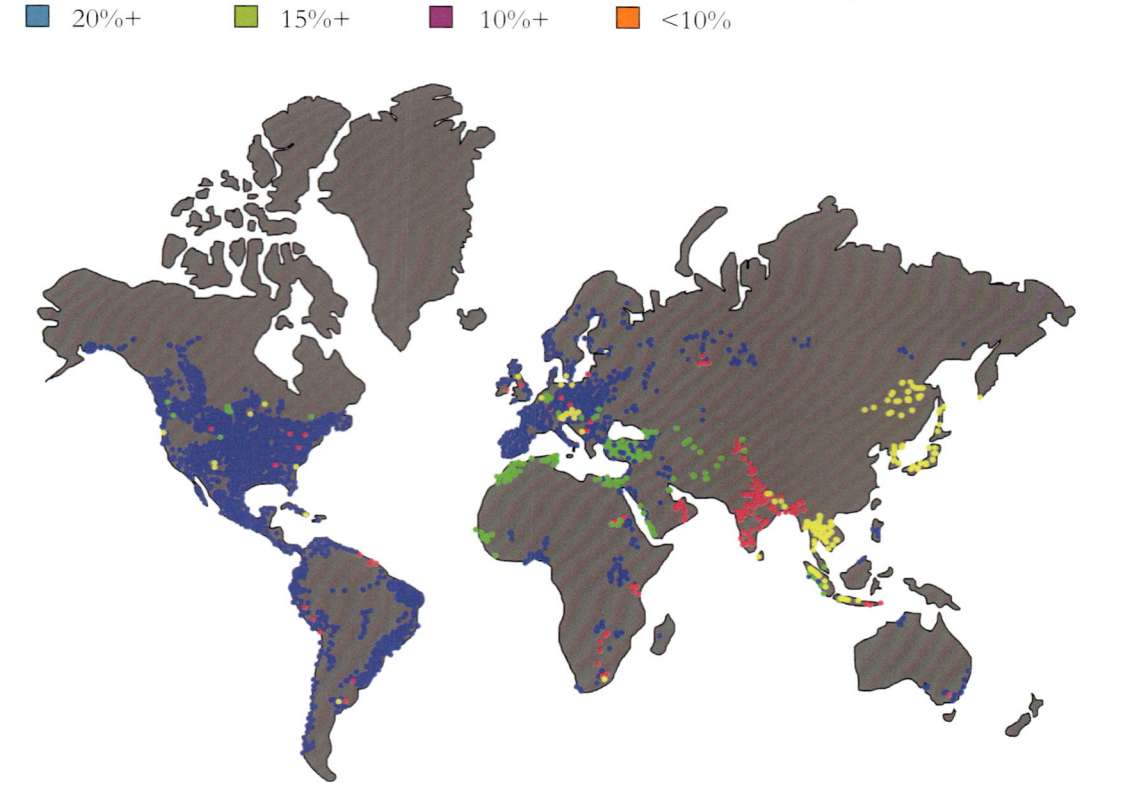

■ 20%+   ■ 15%+   ■ 10%+   ■ <10%

'Google's Geography of Religion' that charts the relative concentration of search terms. For Allah (green), Jesus (blue), Hindu (red), and Buddha (yellow).

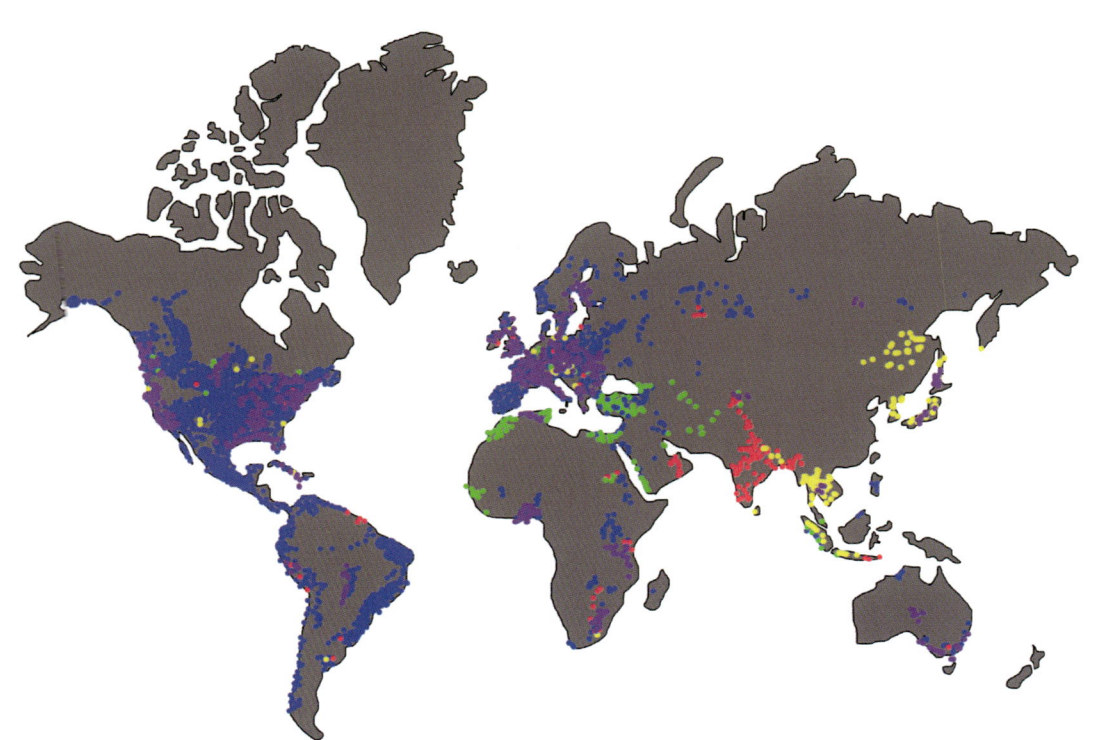

The same map with sex added to the search. For Allah (green), Jesus (blue), Hindu (red), Buddha (yellow) and Sex purple

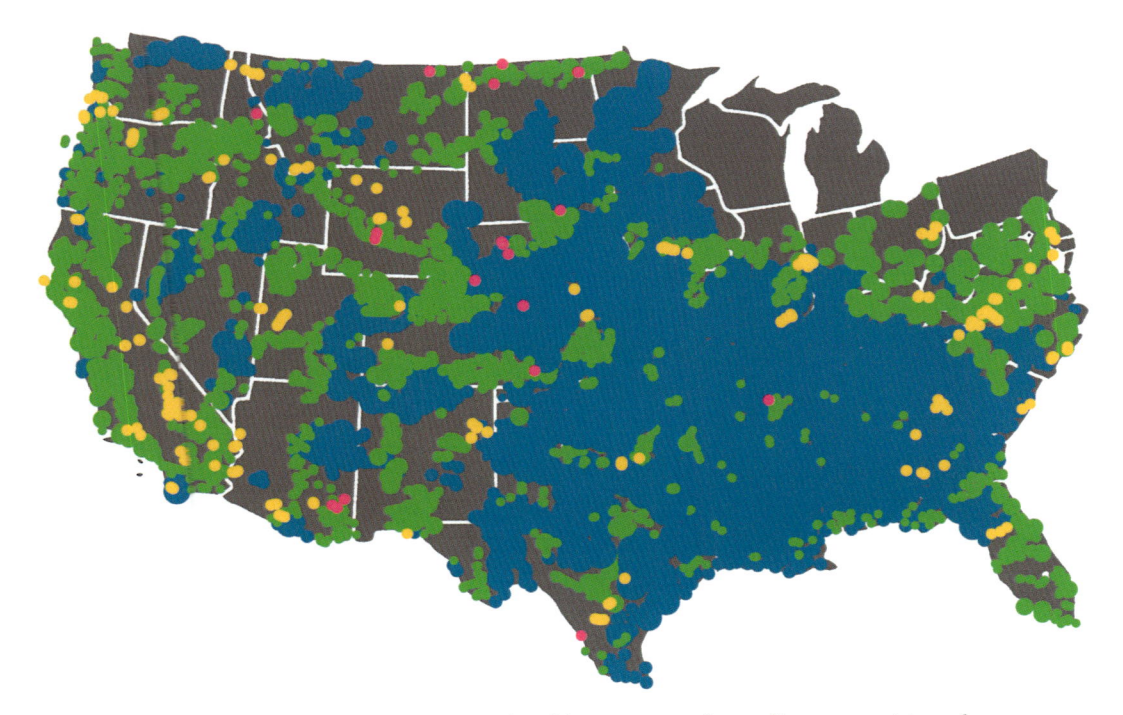

Mapping religion in online realms (or maps) of irreverence that tell us something about our online selves. Blue - more churches; red - more bowling alleys; green - more guns; yellow - more strip clubs

What is your religion 60% 39%

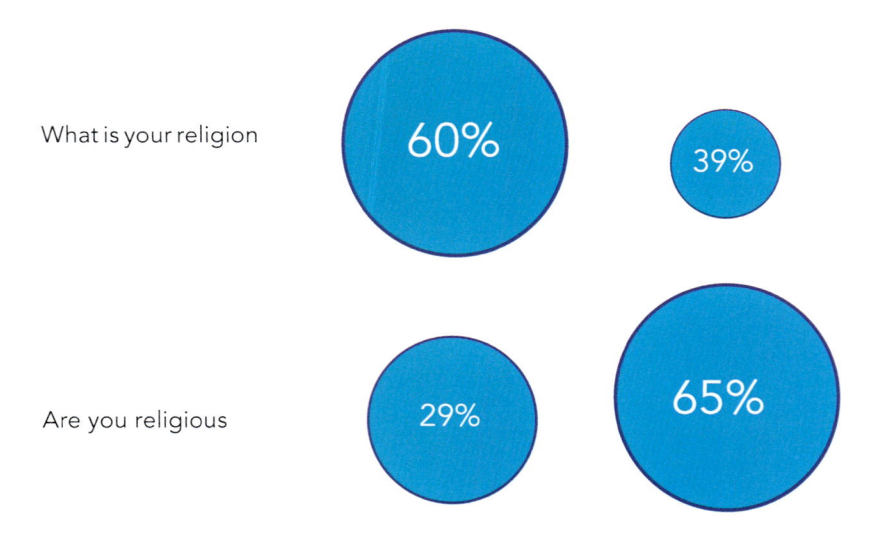

Are you religious 29% 65%

If we were to believe that the wording of a question does not affect the results, it would mean that:

31% of people belong to a religion but are NOT religious
26% of people are NOT religious but belong to a religion

The biased wording of census questions has led to the widespread bet1ef that the UK is a country where the majority of people are practicing Christians

According to March, 2011 YouGov poll

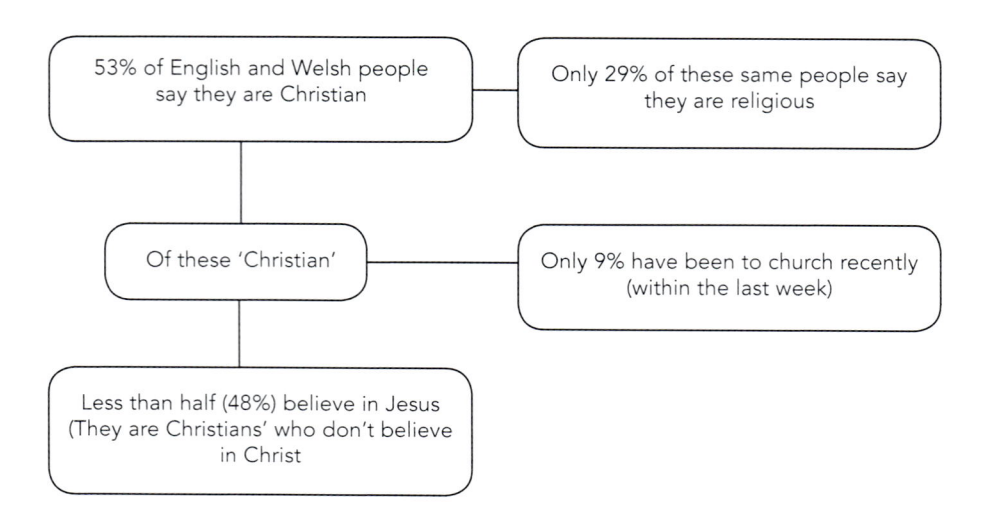

- 53% of English and Welsh people say they are Christian
  - Only 29% of these same people say they are religious
- Of these 'Christian'
  - Only 9% have been to church recently (within the last week)
  - Less than half (48%) believe in Jesus (They are Christians' who don't believe in Christ

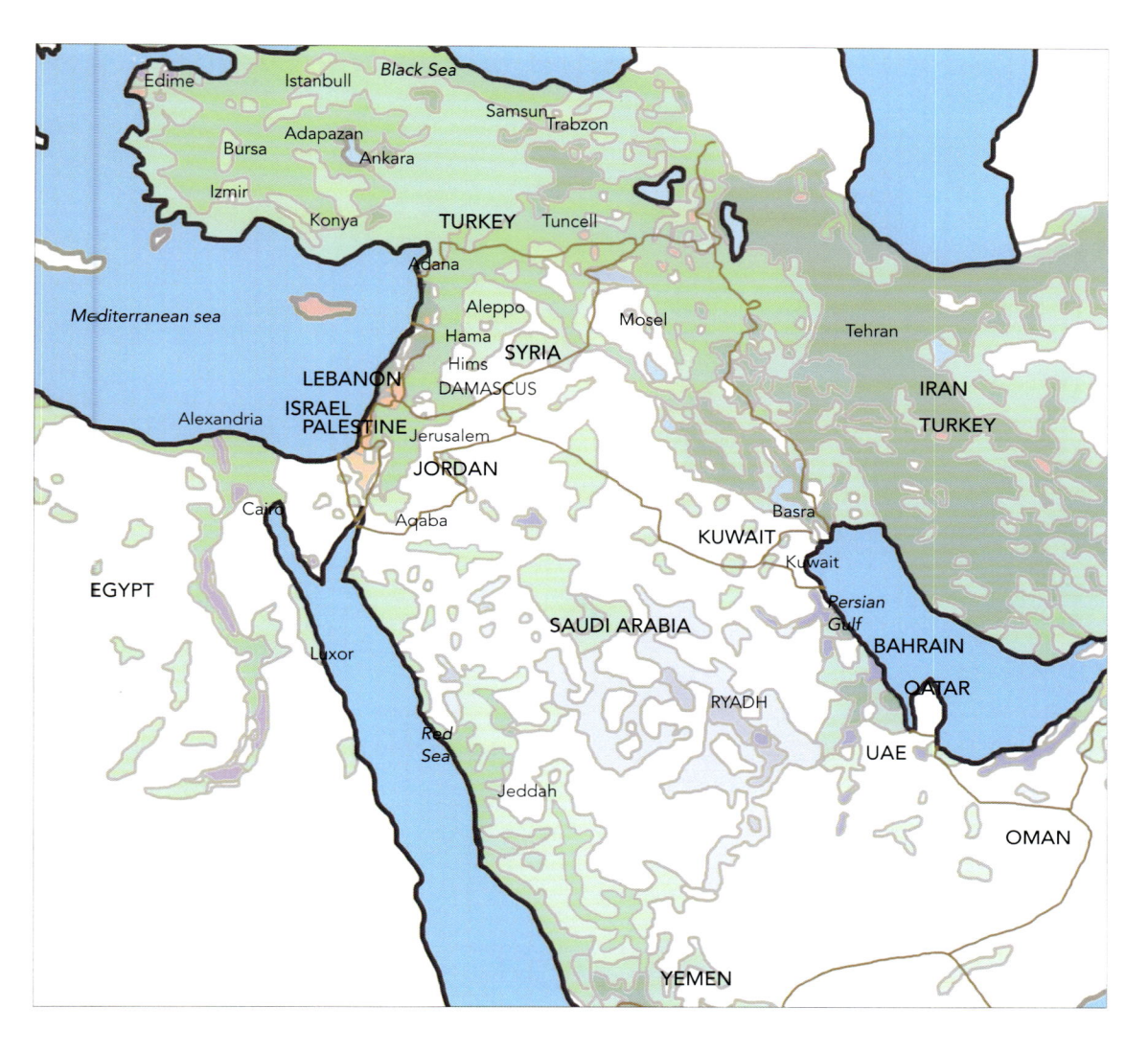

Religious composition of the Middle East

Islam:
- Sunnism (Hanafi, Shafl'I, Maliki and Hanbali rites)
- Shiism (ImamVJa'fari, Zaidi and Isma'ili rites)
- Shiism (Gnostic faiths dissimulating as Shia Islam: Alevism, Alawism, Yarsanism, Zikrism, etc.)
- Ibadism
- Wahhabism (Salafism, Muwahhidun)
- Christianity (various denominations)
- Judaism

Belief held as a result of the accident of where an individual was born

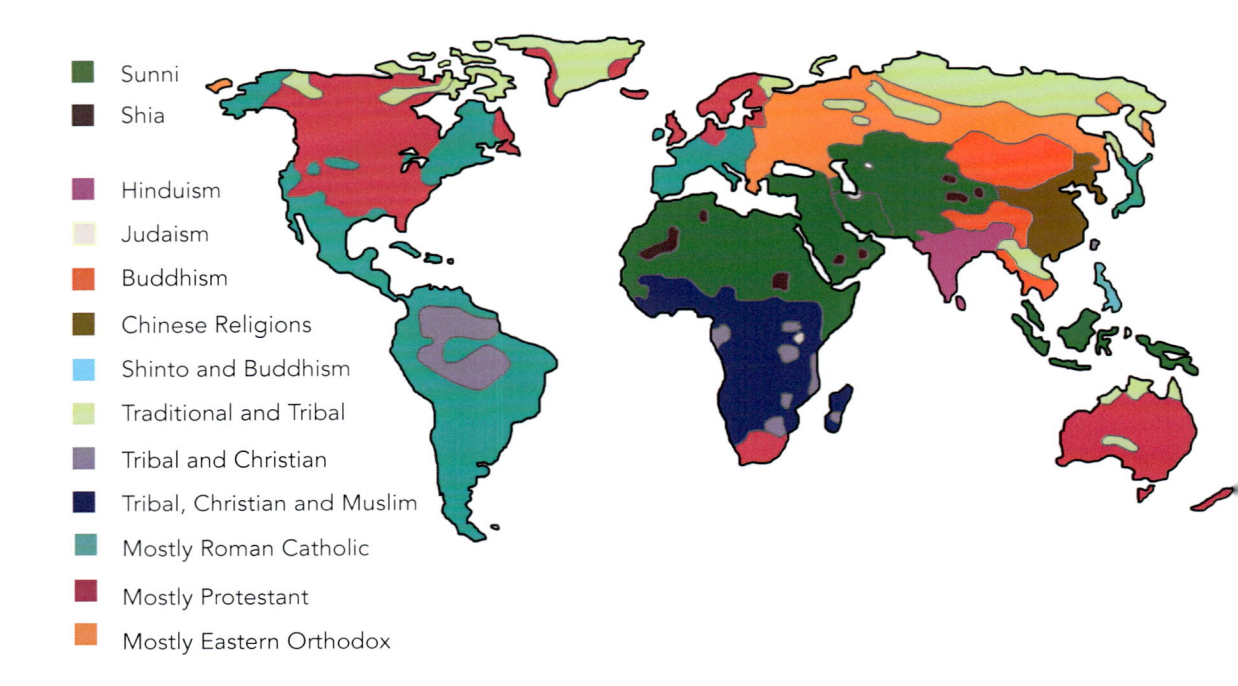

- Sunni
- Shia
- Hinduism
- Judaism
- Buddhism
- Chinese Religions
- Shinto and Buddhism
- Traditional and Tribal
- Tribal and Christian
- Tribal, Christian and Muslim
- Mostly Roman Catholic
- Mostly Protestant
- Mostly Eastern Orthodox

Population reporting no religion, 2011, England and Wales local and unitary authorities

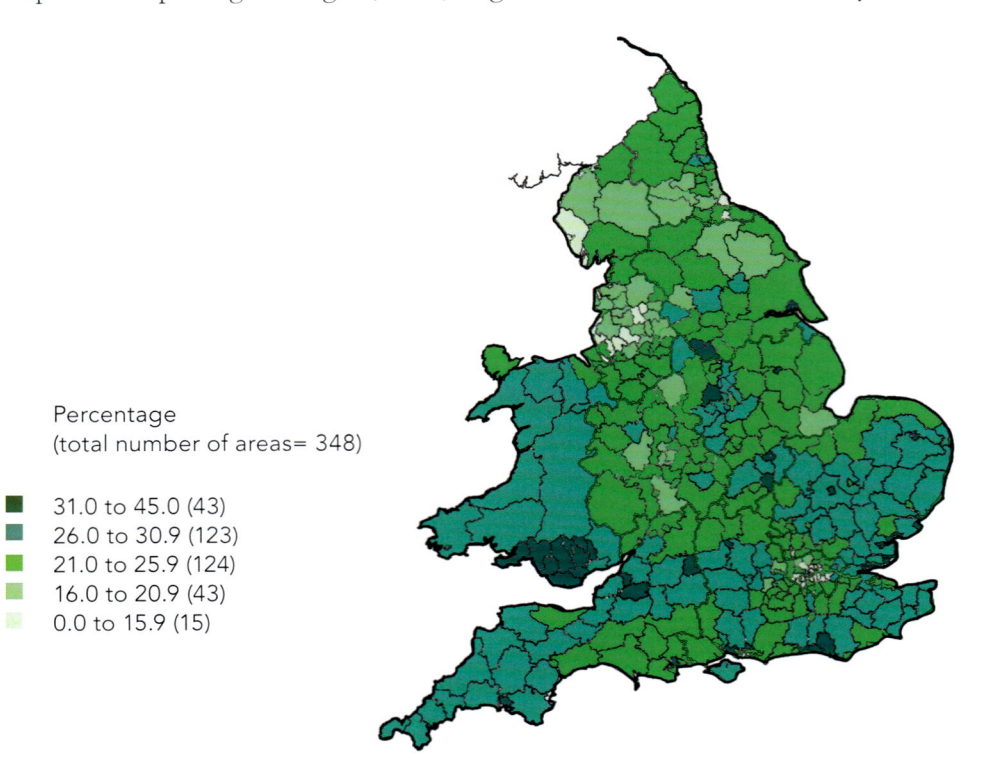

Percentage
(total number of areas = 348)

- 31.0 to 45.0 (43)
- 26.0 to 30.9 (123)
- 21.0 to 25.9 (124)
- 16.0 to 20.9 (43)
- 0.0 to 15.9 (15)

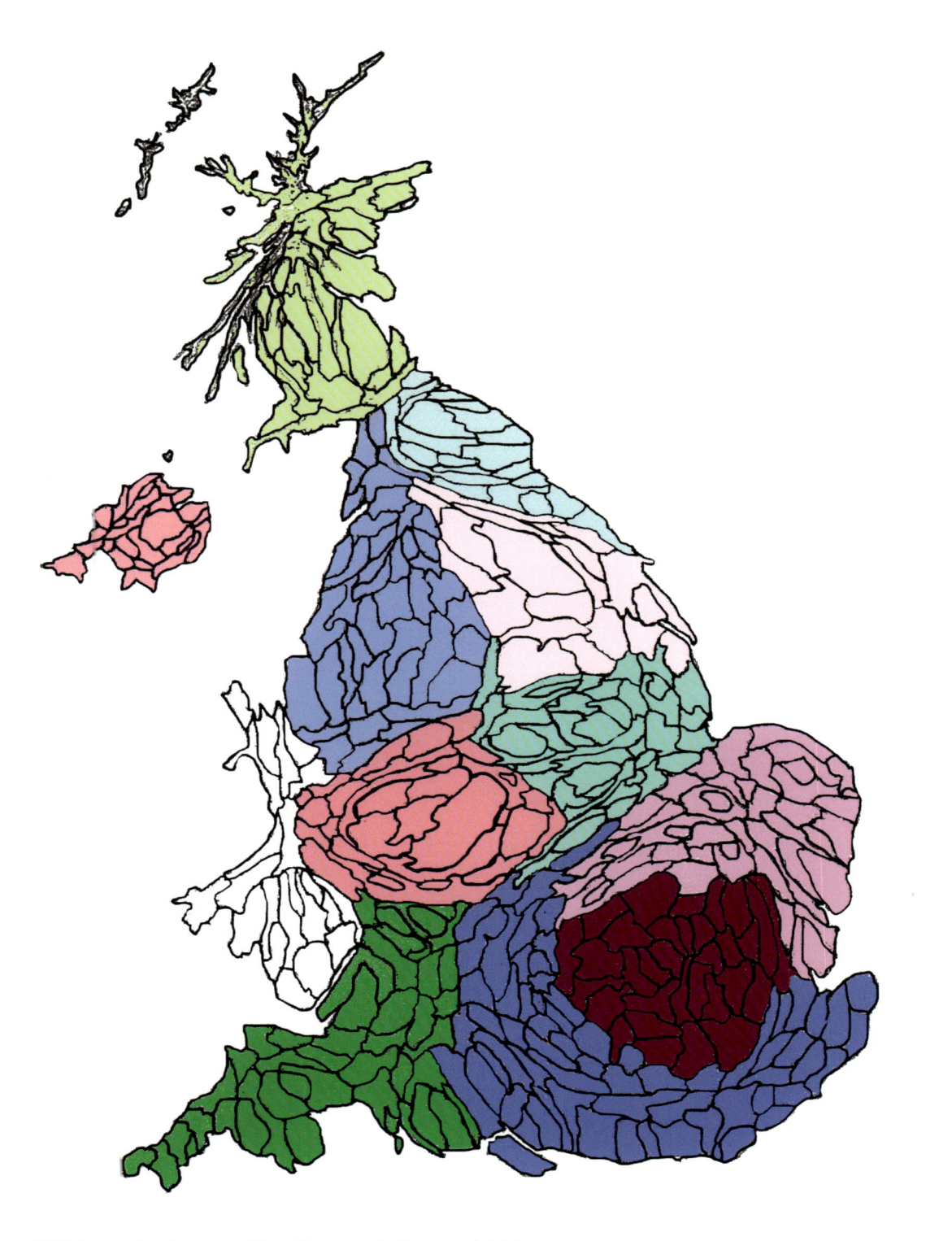

UK Local Authorities: Sized by population aged 85+

Alan (and Eric) in Morcambe looking on the bright side of life - as a humanist

CHAPTER 6
SECULAR GIANTS. *Robert Ingersoll's life, and views on making the best of later life*

There are numerous secular and humanist heroes and heroines - dead and alive - for those of us, whatever our age, who are not religious to draw inspiration, comfort, and re-assurance. As George Melly has written: *As an almost life-long atheist myself, I find it re-assuring to come across others ... as a prop to one's own non-faith.*

Scientists, authors, writers, philosophers; the distinguished and celebrated spokespersons for secular humanism whose writing/broadcasting/oratory we can admire, as well as ordinary folk whose lives can serve as an admirable example to us. (See Luis Granados' book – 'Damned Good Company', for profiles of courageous humanists)

Jen Hancock 'really famous and influential people' who are happy and proud to label themselves as humanists. She categorizes them into **scientists** – Carl Sagan, BF Skinner, Francis Crick and James Watson for example; **writers** – Arthur C Clarke, Kurt Vonnegut and Gore Vidal; **entertainers** – Gene Roddenbury, Steve Allen and Peter Ustinov; **social activists** – Helen Caldicott and Helen Keller. She suggests that if you don't know someone on the list, look them up.

Many of the following are thought to call themselves humanists, (although all too often are not known as such to the public at large:)

Paul Kurtz, Barbara Stoker, Ludovic Kennedy, Bertrand Russell, Lord Hamilton, John Lennon, Woody Allen, Lewis Wolpert, David Hume, Thomas Hardy, Robbie Burns, Thomas Paine, Clare Rainer, Stephen Fry, George Melly, Beatrice and Sydney Webb, Mark Twain, Jonathon Miller, Philip Kitcher, Daniel Dennett, Sam Harris, Christopher Hitchens, Jane Wynne Willson, Phil Zuckerman, Louise Antony, HJ Blackman, Greg Epstein, Alain de Botton, Karen Armstrong, Alom Shaha, Laurie Taylor, Susan Jacoby, AC Grayling, Sherwin Wine, Paul Kurtz, Carl Sagan, Baruch Spinoza, A Phillip Randolph, Bill Gates, Salman Rushdie, Woody Allen, Ibn Warraq, Oprah Winfrey, John Kenneth Galbraith, Mark Twain, Winston Churchill, Jean Paul Sartre, Margaret Meade, Ibn Al-Rawandi, Abu Bakr al-Razi, Jennifer Hancock, Rowan Atkinson, Joseph McCabe, James Joyce, Robert Frost, Thomas Hardy, Thomas Eddison, Sigmund Freud, Virginia Wolf, Kemal Ataturk, Joseph Conrad, Margaret Sanger, Percy Bysshe Shelley, Auguste Comte, Lord Byron, Ralph Vaughan Williams, Thomas Woolston, Simon Bolivar, Epicurus, Gene Kelly, Burt Lancaster, Prmo Levi, Richard Burton, Douglas Adams, Diego Rivera, M N Roy, Irving Berlin, Alfred Hitchcock, Charlie Chaplin, JB Priestley, Luis Bunuel, Margaret Knight, Prof Alice Roberts, Leo Abse, Thomas Aikenhead,

Billy Bragg, Sir Fred Hoyle, Lewis Wolpert, Warren Mitchell, Ernest Haecker, Joey Barton, Angela Eagle MP, Michael Frayn, Baroness Kinnock, Terry Pratchett, Edward Said, Leonard Bernstein, Margaret Kuhn, Alica Roberts, Anthony Pinn, Callum Brown, Peter Derkx, Mathew Engelke, Richard Norman, Isobel Millar.

Who would be YOUR humanist/atheist, agnostic, free thinker of yesteryear or today?

Robert Ingersoll

But what is there about Robert Ingersoll, a nineteenth century American lawyer, agnostic and orator, which makes his life and work so remarkable to be singled out for special admiration, and close consideration? Why choose him over and above, for example, Charles Bradlaugh, in some notable ways his British equivalent? Both men are said to have openly and publicly challenged the Almighty to strike them dead, if he really existed and disproved of atheism!

It is certainly worth noting the contribution of Bradlaugh. As we shall see he was, like Ingersoll, a tireless champion of free thought, a tall well built man, Republican, good humoured, eloquent decent, advocate of birth control, devoted father, supporter of the rights of the oppressed – in his case the Irish and Indians – (Gandhi attended his funeral)a radical though not a socialist. He travelled widely on speaking tours in the UK and USA. His other claim to fame was to be elected as MP for Northampton several times only to be refused permission to take his seat in Parliament as he declined to swear an oath of allegiance to the monarch. He hated hereditary privileges, campaigned to stop rich families like the Churchill's receiving 'perpetual pensions' in return for having undertaken military service for the nation. That appears to have been his only interest in older people!

But, what about the great Ingersoll? Here are some reasons to highlight an admirable man, who I first heard about in 1964 when a student at Bloomington, Indiana (where the bible belt meets the corn belt).

Ingersoll's record

- Despite the excellent recently published biography by Susan Jacoby (to which I am indebted) Ingersoll's contribution to free thought and humanism – especially in America – has often been ignored

- He was an attentive and affectionate family man – and practised what he preached in his private life.

- He straddled the divisions of class, gender and race, and showed an affinity with both city and rural life.

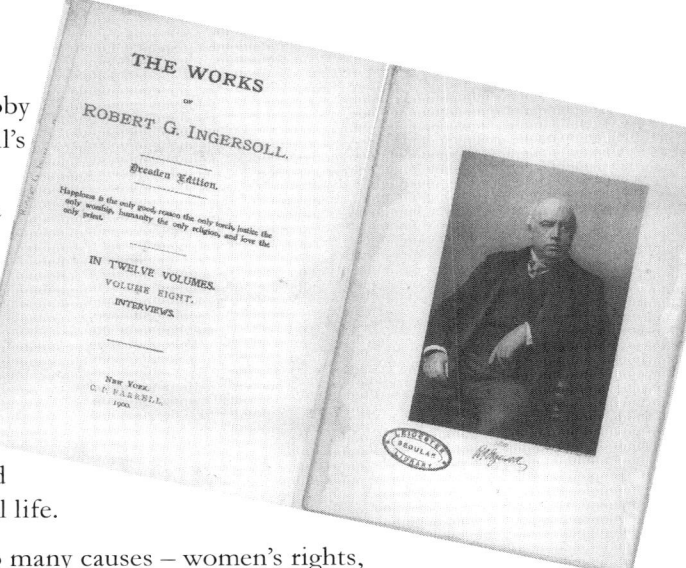

- He campaigned and lectured for so many causes – women's rights, racial equality, birth control, science, freedom of the press, the separation of church and state, republicanism, fair wages for labour (8 hour day for workers) and the right to strike, human love, family life and the arts. He fought against the church and especially religious intolerance and fanaticism, slavery, corporal and capital punishment, pugilism, vivisection, inequality in wealth, narrow patriotism and solitary confinement in prisons.

- He led a full life himself and advocated that older people should also do so. He makes some perceptive suggestions as to how seniors should grow old gracefully and die with dignity.

- He had many personal qualities – kindness, cheerfulness, generosity, open-mindedness, and humour.

- He was convinced by Darwin's theory of evolution –'but only after careful reading'.

- He was unwilling to soften his anti-religious views to gain public office, (some say he could/would have otherwise become President of the US.) He was also able to find common ground with reformed clergy.

- He was a great American humanist – free, frank and forceful. A man who set a great example not only to his contemporaries, but those of us living in a very different world more than a century since his death.

His life and times

Robert was born in 1833, (one of 5 children) in Dresden, near the shores of Lake Seneca in upstate New York. The family moved to Peoria, Illinois on the Mason-Dixon line when he was one year old. He was inseparable from his brother Ebon. His father was a preacher; his mother died aged 36.

He was exposed to religious books at an early age, but also read Shakespeare and Burns. (He could recite 'Holy Willie's Prayer by heart, though not in a Scottish dialect.)

He trained as a lawyer, and was admitted to the bar after learning his trade in an attorney's office. Ingersoll joined the Union army as a colonel in 1861. He was captured but allowed to return home to his young wife Eva, with whom he had two daughters. He practised as a lawyer but declined to see high public office.

Despite an active lifestyle, by his forties, he weighed 200 pounds.

He was greatly in demand as a public speaker.(Many of his public and after – dinner speeches, eulogies etc are to be found in the 12 volume edition of his collected works which are available in the library of Conway Hall, London). Between 1875 and his death, he spoke in every state except Mississippi, North Carolina and Oklahoma. His 'gospel of humanity and happiness' attracted huge paying audiences who appreciated his dry and acerbic humour, colloquial turn of phrase and weighty authority.

Farmers, mechanics and labourers flocked to hear him. His audiences consisted 'half of ladies'. Mrs Anna Brooks, a Texan rancher's wife rode more than 30 miles on horseback in 1896 to hear Ingersoll's speech on the 'Liberty of man, woman and child' in the town of Sherman (population 9,000) (Jacoby)

His work was translated into Yiddish. He gave an address to 'the coloured people' in Galesburg in 1867. He travelled to Burns' birthplace in Ayshire, Scotland – despite having an avowed aversion to Britain's old world system of royalty, colonialism and class system.

He was known to his clerical enemies as 'Robert Injuresoul'. His wealth and expansive lifestyle attracted criticism. Reporters tried, in vain, to find salacious stories about his personal life.

His contemporary friends, allies and (later) admirers included Mark Twain; Clarence Darrow; WC Fields, HL Mencken; Andrew Carnegie; and Walt Whitman 'Wahoo' Sam Crawford (a famous baseball players). Philo D Beckwith (a progressive employee and maker of stoves and furnaces in Dowagiac, Michigan); Eugene Debs (Socialist candidate for the presidency in 1920), who first heard him speak in Terra Haute, Indiana and rode all the way by train to Cincinnati with Robert Ingersoll to enable them to converse at length, according to Susan Jacoby, Frederick Douglass, (an eminent leader of the seven million Americans of the day).

In later years he lived in Washington and New York – which he preferred due to its livelier cultural life. His parties were very popular.

He spent the last month of his life at the home of his daughter Eva at Dobbs Ferry, overlooking the Hudson River in New York. He died on 21st July, 1899. He had spent the previous evening playing billiards with his brother in law. He had a cigar on the porch and was heard to remark – 'This is a beautiful world.' (Jacoby).

He was very anxious to show that he underwent no deathbed religious conversion. As Matthew d'Ancona has written in relation to Christopher Hitchins - 'It is not uncommon for religions to claim deathbed conversion on the part of non-believers. The faithful have form when it comes to salsifying deathbed conversions! Ingersoll's body was cremated and remains, together with those of his wife who died in 1923, in Arlington National cemetery.

Ingersoll's sayings:

'I want brain without a chain';
'judge me by deed not creed';
Sabbaths used to be prisons – every Sunday a bastille;
No man of humour ever founded a religion – never;
I believe in the gospel of good living, good clothes, good houses;
the school house is my cathedral;
I believe the gospel of humanity is the grand religion;
What do you propose in place of all this (they ask me) – good fellowship, mutual respect, forbearance.

He thought deeply what might be … in *IF* he wrote:

If cathedrals had been universities
If dungeons of the inquisition had been labs
If Christians had believed in character instead of creed
If they had taken from the Bible only that what is good
And thrown away the wicked and absurd
If temple domes had been observatories

If priests had been philosophers
If missionaries had taught useful arts instead of bible lore
If astrology had been astronomy
If the black arts had been chemistry
If superstition had been science
If religion had been humanity
The world would then be a heaven
Filled with love, and liberty, and joy

You had better live well and die cursing than live badly and die praying.

I cannot see why we should expect an infinite god to do better in another world than he does in this one.

In a letter to his grandchildren in February 1898 he wrote:

Dear Eva and Robbie,
We are glad that you love us and want us to come home. We will see you in a few days, and tell you where we have been and what we have seen. We have seen thousands of men, women and children and lots of babes. But we have seen no girl or boy as sweet as you.

This is a beautiful day and Grandma and I are going to take a walk. The sun is shining and the sky is as blue as Robbie's eyes and as bright as Eva's smile. We love you both and would like to hug and kiss you this morning. I hope you had a good dream last night. We hope your dolls and animals are well – and no legs broken. As soon as I get home I will eat some baked apples with you and give you lots of whipped cream. We will have a gay time.

Well goodbye. Love and kisses to you both. Your letters make me happy.

Grandma and Grandpa

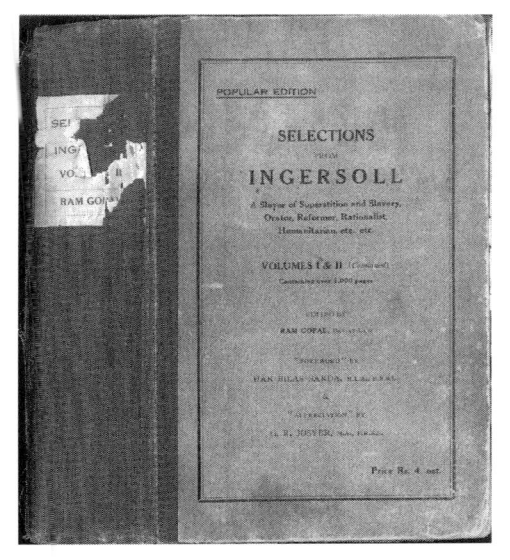

Ingersoll's 'Happiness creed' as recorded for posterity in Thomas Eddison's lab and can be heard in RI's Dresden modest birthplace museum. (Jacoby).

'Happiness is the only good. The time to be happy is now. The place to be happy is here. The way to be happy is to make others so'.

He was a progressive thinker as evidenced by his assertion – 'It is far cheaper to build school houses than prisons, and much better to have scholars than convicts' (Jacoby)

- Between 1869 and 1899 Ingersoll toured the nation almost continuously, delivering six or seven lectures a week to sold out houses.
- Though a formidable orator and likeable character, Ingersoll is largely forgotten today. Jacques Berlinerblau

Ingersoll's remarks on ageing

- The old man has been long at the fair. He is acquainted with the jugglers at the booths. His curiosity has been satisfied. He looks through the glitter and the gloss. To conduct, manners, theories, philosophies – he sees more clearly. The light shines in his eyes.

- An old man imagines – that everything was better when he was young, that the weather could be depended on; that sudden changes were recent inventions; that people used to be honest; that grocers gave full weight and merchants full measure; he mistakes the twilight of his own years for the coming of the night of universal decay and death; he imagines what has happened to him has happened to the world.

- It does not occur to him that millions, at the moment he is talking, are undergoing the experiences of his youth, and that when they become old, they will praise the very days that he denounces. The garden of Eden has always been behind us. The golden age, after all, is the memory of youth. It is the result of remembered pleasure In the midst of present pain. In fact there were horrible old times – Krupp guns, slavery upheld, imprisonment for debts, crimes punishable by death, the insane treated like wild beasts, no respect was paid to sex or AGE

- I would make Sunday more useful and cheerful. I would turn it into a holiday, a day of zest and peace, a day to get acquainted with your wife and children, a day to exchange civilities with your neighbours. I would see the church changed to a place of entertainment, see Sunday school changed to a happy dance on the village green.

- It is a splendid thing that the woman you really love will never grow old to you. Through the wrinkles of time, through the mask of years, if you really love her, you will always see the face you loved and won. A woman who really loves a man does not see that he grows old; he is not decrepit to her; she always sees the same gallant gentleman who won her hand and heart …

Question: *How have you acquired the art of growing old gracefully?*
Answer: *Some people hang on to a many good years, but they hardly can be said to do much real living. Regular habits have their place, but variety can be a great relief.*

If we could only keep from being annoyed at little things, it would add to the luxury of living. It's a great thing to have an object in life, something to work for and think for. If a man only thinks of himself, his own comfort, his own importance, he will not grow old gracefully. Probably the best medicine in the world, is to make someone happy. Those who take an interest in what they see, and keep their minds busy are always young. As long as a man lives he should study. … The intelligent, the kind, the reasonably contented, the courageous, grow old gracefully.

There is no sweeter way to end life as in peace on a farm. In the quiet of the country, out of the mad race for money, place and power, out of the dusty highways where fools struggle and strive for the hollow praise of other fools, surrounded by pleasant fields and faithful friends, by those I have loved, I hope to end my days, to pass away serenely as the autumn.

Someone to cherish

Robert Ingersoll was likeable, formidable, and inspirational. He is woefully neglected in North America, despite the recent attempt by Susan Jacoby to remind the world who he was, what he did and said. His contribution to 19th century secular thought, and worthy progressive causes which he so ably espoused, is remarkable. Whilst modern humanism has its leading lights, few, if any, can equal the talents of Ingersoll in the breadth of his thought and powers of communication. Isn't it time for his life to be celebrated in a Hollywood blockbuster, along with others such as Thomas Paine and Frederick Douglass? Despite rampant, right-wing tendencies apparent in modern American politics and culture, it is worth reminding ourselves that there is also a long American radical tradition to be lauded, and no where more so than in the example set by Robert Ingersoll.

Robert Ingersoll. Apparently on one of his lecture tours in Texas south west A rancher's wife - Anna Brooks rode 30 miles on horseback to a place called Sherman (pop. 9000) to hear him speak.

CHAPTER 7
THE PEPPERED MOTH: *let's hear it for Charles Darwin, and tell our grandchildren about evolution and explain diversity in the world*

The great Charles Darwin

Charles Darwin's life, work, contribution to science, and role in questioning traditional (religious) views on the world and the evolution of humanity, has been well documented. He revealed and partly explained the glorious complexity of life.

His upbringing, education, five year journey round the world on the Beagle, meticulous research, caution in publishing his revolutionary theory on evolution by natural selection, collaboration with Alfred Russell Wallace, ill health and family tragedies, phenomenal research output, and national acclaim are all well known. *On the Origin of Species* continues to be reprinted and translated. For the time being he appears on the back of the British £10 pound note. Modern scientists use his work as a template and fill in the gaps in his knowledge. Creationists deny that he was right, indeed they continue to maintain that evolution is a fraud. Most people, (in the west at least) including many Christians and other religious believers, today accept his basic treatise. Humanists see him as a scientific hero, who broke the dictates of faith-inclined naturalists in the mid 19th century and led the way for scientific rationality to hold sway in thought, education, and research. As AC Grayling has noted – *he completely re-drew mankind's intellectual map*. He 'threw light' – one of his favourite expressions - on how competition and a changing environment can forge new species, if so little was known in his lifetime about genes and evolutionary theory and genetics. The regret is that in today's crowded curriculum and instant celebrity culture, Darwin may be forgotten. How many people for example celebrate Darwin Day or visit his house in Kent or memorial in Westminster Abbey?

Darwin studied many creatures – finches, mice, worms, shellfish, pigeons … but not as far as we know the peppered moth – sometimes called *Darwin's moth*. He did not know it at the time, but the rapid evolution of the peppered moth was happening in his lifetime – in 'real' time, not numbers of years – in the industrial cities not far from where he was born.

The Darwins and Down House

Charles Darwin, as well as being an extraordinary Victorian scientist, was a family man. Most of his life was spent at Down House, near the village of Downe in Kent. Here he wrote *On the Origin of Species* (taking 13 months and 10 days), did many experiments in later life, played with his children, entertained their visitors. Down House is now a UNESCO World Heritage site, and it surely should be. It is owned, operated by English Heritage as a busy attraction for 'pilgrims' from home and abroad.

Charles Darwin's life and character are to be glimpsed in the rooms, artefacts and garden of this secular shrine.

He was a sensitive and modest man. He was attentive to his wife and children, conciliatory to his peers (more so than Huxley), respectful to his employers ('would you be so good as to' … was his way of asking his staff to do something), a lover of the English countryside, a committed member of the local community (for many years he was treasurer of Downe Friendly Society), an avid reader of scientific treatises and novels, a genial host, and a loving husband and father.

His work and family life kept him busy. All this while suffering bouts of illness throughout his later life. Exactly what his ailments were is unclear. Maybe a tropical disease caught on this travels on the *Beagle*, possibly an element of stress was involved. But he certainly suffered painful days and sleepless nights. The 'water-cures' he enthusiastically embraced, proved of little lasting value.

The tragic loss of three children, and especially their lively daughter, Annie was a terrible blow. 'We have lost the joy she …..and the solace of our old age' he wrote.

Most pictures of Charles Darwin show him as a solemn, bearded, elderly man. One can discern the full family life the Darwins enjoyed from a visit to their home. His study and books, greenhouse and walks, all attest to his serious work and happy social life.

I have abiding memories of a visit to Down House. Talking to two older women volunteer gardeners in the rain, listening to Sir David Attenborough's commentary, and observing the polished wooden slide on the main stairs, which had been made for the Darwin children to play indoors on rainy days.

If you haven't been to Down House, then make sure you go soon and maybe take your grandchildren. You will surely have an enjoyable and informative day - as many thousands do every year. His bedroom, recently recreated, has just been opened to the public. You can use your senior bus pass to get there. Some record their experience on Trip Advisor.

> Trip Advisor: 294 reviews of which 153 excellent, 103 very good, 27 average, 6 poor, 5 terrible.
>
> **Comments on a visit to Down House**:
> A hidden treasure
> A really good day out
> Poignantly homely
> Glimpses of Victorian life
> Best on a late afternoon in summer
> Showed what a free thinking and loving parent he was.
> A fabulous memorial to a very great man
> An informative pilgrimage
> Great garden for children to play in
> Nice cake in the café
> Tucked away in the Kentish countryside
> Hard to get to but so very worth it
> Study just as if Darwin had popped out
> Enlightening - a special place

The Peppered Moth

The peppered moth (Biston betularia) is often cited as a classic textbook example of evolution by natural selection. Why? Because the basic story is easy to understand, it has happened in a relatively short period of time and the evidence in support of the story is overwhelming.

The *International Wildlife Encyclopedia* states, 'This is the most striking evolutionary change ever to have been witnessed by man.'

Yet there are those who question the very idea and case study. In 1999 one national British newspaper's headline, *Scientists pick holes in Darwin moth theory*, and article, claimed that the rise and fall of the peppered moth was – 'based on a series of scientific blunders'. The Centre for Science and Culture Discovery Institute referred to 'moth-eaten statistics', Darwinism in a 'Flutter' and 'the Piltdown moth'. There were even accusations of fraud by Judith Hooper in her book *Of Moths and Men*.

Such criticisms have been dismissed by serious scientists as 'quasi-assessments of the evidence', 'flimsy conspiracy theory', 'smearing a brilliant naturalist'. Coyne concludes – the creationists have tried to refute evolution itself and 'by peddling innuendo and failing to distinguish clearly the undeniable fact of selection from the contested agent of selection, Hooper has done the scientific community a disservice'. Finally in a brochure entitled *Why I believe in Creation* by Dr Monty White we find the following statement – 'this proves nothing about evolution – the moths are still the same species of moths, and in both varieties were, and still are, being produced'.

When, where and how the moth evolved

So what is the story of the evolution of the peppered moth that would have overjoyed Charles Darwin and which we can recount with enthusiasm to our children and grandchildren?

Studies have shown that in the English countryside the typical moth with pale and speckled coloured wings thrived. Resting during the day on trees it was well camouflaged on the light coloured lichens growing on birch and other trees. Hungry birds such as robins, nuthatches and hedge sparrows might miss this juice prey. But come the industrial revolution and the pall of pollution thrown out from the chimney stacks of cotton and woollen mills, these pale creatures stood out against the sooty bark of trees located in and downwind from industrial heartlands. They were spotted and eaten, certainly ahead of a second and darker type of peppered moth – Carboneria, which up to that time were relatively few in number.

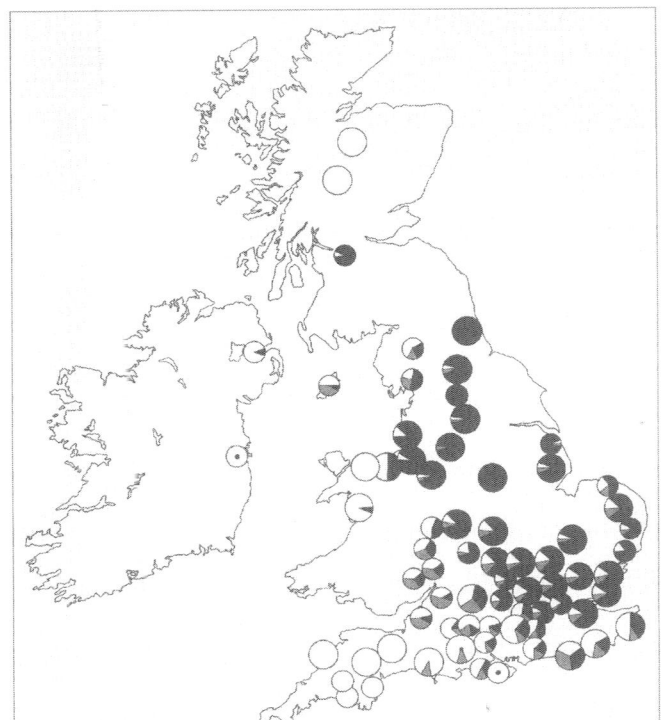

Distribution of the Peppered Moth

Within a short time pale moths had all but disappeared in urban Lancashire, and the Midlands. It was the darker variety that fitted into this new environment, were less conspicuous, were less likely to spotted by predators and 'survived'. Indeed they did more than that – in 1848 the first black-winged moth was spotted in Manchester, but by 1900 the ratio of dark to light moths in Manchester was 99:1. In areas close by, where pollution was spread by prevailing winds, the population of the dark Carbonaria never dropped to below 80%. In rural areas such as the south west of England, it was the pale moth which still held sway, because in unpolluted areas it survived better than its darker 'cousin' up t'north.

Industrial melanism is the term given to these striking evolutionary changes and natural selection producing adaptation in accordance with Darwin's theory.

But the story doesn't end there. With the de-industrialisation and the passage of the clean air legislation in the 1950s in the UK, another change was noted by scientists observing the prevalence of the peppered moth populations at different times and in varied locations.

Scientists have found that there has been a steep decline in the numbers and proportion of dark moths, especially in now less polluted industrial areas where they previously held sway. One biologist goes as far as to state that dark moths face an uncertain future in Britain in the 21st century. One source has even estimated that by 2019 dark moths will comprise only 1% of the declining population. With less pollution - 'lighter' tree bark foliage - the darker moth is predated and the lighter one is well camouflaged and survives/thrives.

That the peppered moths of different colour have survived better or worse at different times and in different times there can be no doubt. Meticulous research backs up these changing evolutionary patterns correlating with environmental changes. Those that have escaped the attention of birds, have bred and passed on their traits to their young. Selective predation, the most common process at work, is widely accepted by scientists.

Similar research has been undertaken on other species, for example the walking stick insect on the hills of California, mice on the Gulf Coast of Florida.

The peppered moth as a classic case of evolution by natural selection is admirably analysed and illustrated in several books. Some science textbooks note how this particular species has adapted to its changing environment. Others are entirely devoted to outlining the experiments which have been conducted into the temporal and spatial elements of this example of evolution in our lifetime and on our doorstep. Hopi Hoekstra of Harvard University found that beach mice have paler coats than mice living on the mainland. This camouflages them better on pale sand: owls, hawks and herons eat more of the poorly disguised mice, leaving the others to breed. She has traced the colour difference to the change of a single letter in a single gene, which cuts down the production of pigment in the fur. The mutation was caused since the beach islands formed less than 6,000 years ago.

The father of evolution would be thrilled to see the science his theory has inspired. In the beak of the finch, and the fur of the mouse (as well as the wings of the peppered moth) we can actually see the process of natural selection at work, moulding and modifying the DNA of genes and their expression to adapt the organism to its particular circumstances. Matt Ridley

I personally have only ever seen two peppered moths — one in rural Scotland and the other in the Cotswolds — both were settled on white surfaces of buildings and both had pale speckled wings. I saw them clearly but apparently they were missed by hungry sparrows nearby. I use Darwin's masterpiece as a scaffold rather than a straight jacket. Steve Jones

Darwin would be overjoyed to see how much he did not know, and how much we have yet to learn. David Quammen

200 years of selective snacking   TT

❦ The main lesson from biogeography is that only evolution can explain the diversity of life.

❦ Maybe the real lesson of the fluctuating fortunes of the peppered moth in the UK during the last two hundred years is that you don't have to have gone to the Gallapagos islands with Charles Darwin or travel the world to see the evidence of evolution in all its extraordinary variety and complexity.

❦ The distribution of life on earth reflects a blend of chance and lawfulness. Chance because the dispersal of animals and plants depends on unpredictable vagaries such as winds, currents, and the opportunity to colonize. Lawfulness … evolutionary theory predicts that many animals and plants arriving in new and unoccupied habitats will evolve to thrive there, and will form new species, filling up ecological niches.

Jerry Coyne

These words by leading scientists show how Darwin is held in high esteem. He certainly did not know all the mechanics and processes of evolution, including the intricacies of genetics which are only now being fully understood. In essence, his research and writing remains a central pillar in the understanding of our world. Let's tell our grandchildren about him and the peppered moth.

Want to know more about the peppered moth? Here is some reading.

A Handbook of Evolution. The British Museum, 1959

The Mechanics of Evolution. W H Dowdeswell, Heinemann, 1963

The Evolution of Melanism by B Kettlewell Clarendn Press 1973

Science. Unit 19 *Life and Evolution,* Unit 20 *Inheritance and cell division,* and Unit 21 *Genes and Evolution.* The Open University, 1987

Melanism: Evolution in Action by M Majerus. Oxford University Press, 1998

Fine Tuning the Peppered Moth Paradigm by Bruce Grant in *Evolution,* 1999, pages 980-984

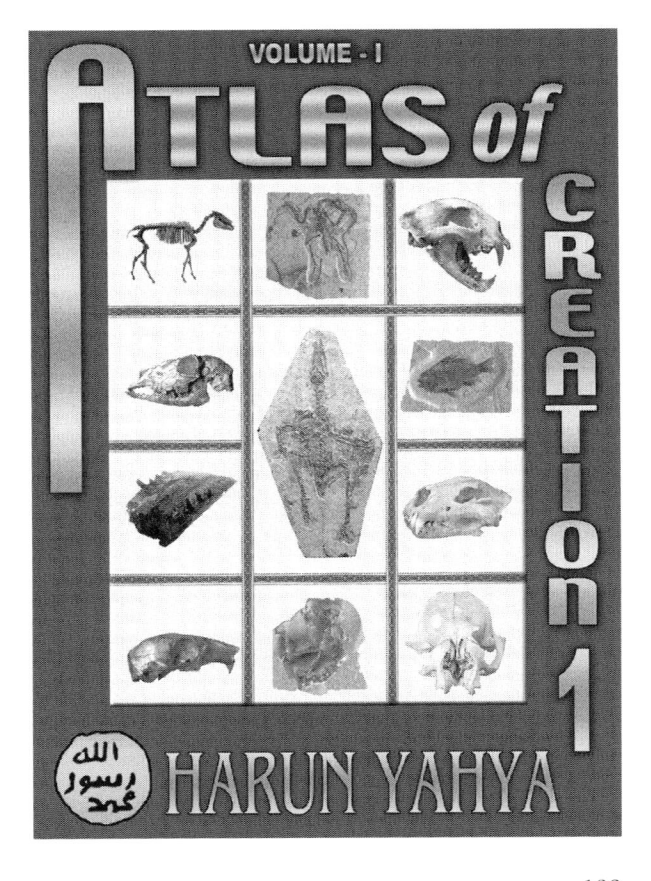

Charles Darwin and evolution. *Read all about it*

There are numerous books and other publications about the wonderful life and work of this celebrated scientist. They include:

- *Charles Darwin*, John Chancellor. Book club Associates, 1973. Readable and amply illustrated.

- *Darwin's Ghosts*, Rebecca Stott. Records the contributions of those who preceded Darwin in his search for an understanding of how life on earth developed.

- *The Illustrated Origin of the Species*, Charles Darwin abridged and introduced by Richard Leakey. Book club Associates, 1979. Another classic. Section on the peppered moth with photographs and a good map – pages 30-32

- *Autobiography of Charles Darwin*. Thinker's Library Nr 7, (with two appendices by son Sir Francis Darwin). 1929

- *Annie's Box : Charles Darwin, his Daughter and Human Evolution*. Randall Keynes, 2001

- *Darwin's Luck: chance and fortune in the life and work of Charles Darwin*. Patrick Armstrong, 2009

- Darwin. Portrait of a Genius. Paul Johnson, Viking, 2012

- *Darwin and the Beagle,* Alan Moorhead. Penguin Books , 1969 Well written and illustrated

- *Charles Darwin,* Cyril Aydon. Constable, 2002 A well written, all round account of his life and work – postscript – a backward look provides some first class insights into Darwin's contribution to science and evolutionary theory and research.

- *Darwin. A Life in Poems*. Ruth Padel, 2009

- *The Young Charles Darwin*. Keith Thomson, 2009. Good analysis of his formative years

- *Evolution. The Triumph of an Idea*. Especially part one, Carl Zimmer, 2002. A monumental work, beautifully illustrated.

- *Darwin … off the record*. Watkins Publishing, 2010. This pocket book probes behind some key issues in his life in a series of fictional interviews.

- *Darwin and Evolution for Kids*, Kristan Lawson. Includes numerous illustrations and activities to engage readers – young and old?

- *Darwin – A Graphic Biography,* Simon Gurr and Eugene Byrne. BCDP, 2009. A humorous and slightly bizarre 'comic' book.

- *Darwin for Beginners,* Jonathon Miller and Borin Van Loon. Icon Books, 1992. Some good cartoons and commentary.

- *Darwin and Evolution for Kids. His Life and Ideas,* Kristan Lawson. Chicago Review Press 2003. Useful book for children, with a good summary of the peppered moth as an example of evolution in action.

- *Darwin's First Clues,* David Quammen. *Modern Darwins,* Matt Ridley, David Quamman. *National Geographic,* vol 215, 2009

- Also a useful resource for schools - *A Whisper to a Shout,* a resources project on the peppered moth and evolution. Manchester School of Art.

- For ideas about presentations to schools by grandparents) contact Sonia.vidal@gmail.com or Claudia_bradshaw@yahoo.co.uk

---

Perhaps the best scientific book on evolution, which also highlights Darwin's theoretical and practical work and contribution is Jerry Coyne's, *Why Evolution is True.*

Treasured objects

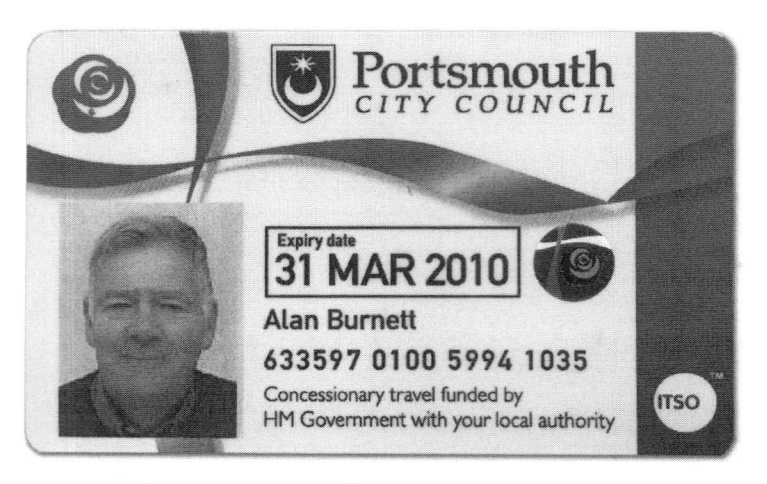

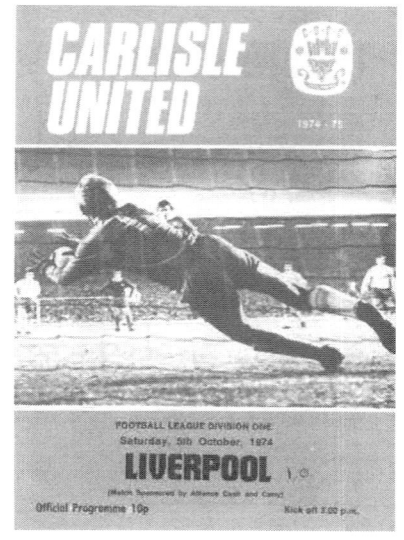

CHAPTER 8
SPECIAL OBJECTS, PEOPLE, PLACES, EVENTS: CLEVER (CHURCH) CONVERSIONS

For older sceptics there are objects/ possessions, people, places, past events which can provide satisfaction and solace in our daily live. Music, books and TV programmes to enjoy. Here are a few of my suggestions to help us enjoy later life.

Objects (not a crucifix)

We all have treasured personal belongings that we cherish and enjoy having around us. Items that were familiar to us as children and influenced our lives and careers, e.g. vinyl records. Family photographs and heirlooms, childhood possessions, our children's toys and books, jewellery that has sentimental value, paintings and books, souvenirs from afar, items that are placed on our mantelpiece or on our window sills, or hidden away for safety in locked cupboards. Cues to reminiscence in later life. Possessions that 'we can't take with us when we die' but may wish to pass on to our nearest and dearest.

For me, my treasured possessions include my dad's old Bakelite radio and mum's sugar bowl, copies of Charles Darwin's and Robert Ingersoll's books (not first editions) jazz records from the 60s, 2008 FA Cup final ticket and scarf, an antique Frisbee, Carr's biscuit tin, Phd thesis, maps galore. **Here are a few - what about yours?**

Blue Note 78 RPM jazz records

People (unlikely to be priests)

There are people we know and/or remember with love, affection, admiration, respect, gratitude....They inspired, encouraged, and sustained us. Our parents, family, siblings, teachers, and mentors who made such a difference to our lives. Musicians and artists whose work inspires us. Loved ones – dead or alive. People whose company we enjoy/enjoyed – and miss most days. Rebels who stood up for what they believed in, and spent much of their time improving the lives of others. Naturalists, like David Attenborough who have shown us the wonderful diversity of the world.

These are some of the heroes– but there are many more - who have inspire(d) me. What about you?

With Jenny in Durham  *B.B. King*  *Eddie Izzard*  *David Attenborough*

George Melly & friends  *Tom, Kate and Helen*

The late Jo Cox  *Mr Philipp*  *Nelson Mandela*

Places (rarely holy sites)

There are special places where we were brought up, feel we belong, love to visit, bring us joy, and to spend time in; can recall with clarity and sometimes dream about. Maybe we would like to have our ashes scattered there. Sea sides and coastlines, rivers/streams, and lakes, forests, meadows and hedgerows with wild flowers, parks and public gardens, streets and houses where we grew up, gardens and parks, bookshops, bars and restaurants, jazz clubs and concert halls, cathedrals and churches, libraries and views of favourite landscapes. These 'favourite' places have their sights, smells and sounds which bring back happy memories. (See *My favourite place - a tribute to Scotland's best-loved places,* published by Scottish Book Trust

Mine include the Tavistock Square Peace Park; the South Bank in London, between Festival Hall and Tate Modern; Brunton and Fratton Parks; Wisley walled garden; Wasdale and Buttermere in the Lake District. The Pheasant Inn at Bassenthwaite and the Royal Oak at Langstone; Durham Cathedral; Watts Coffee Shop and Edenside Cricket ground in Carlisle; the River Eden and the south coast of the Isle of Wight. The A3 and A232; Hadrian's Wall, Portchester Castle, the Grand Canyon and Baja California.

Which places are special to you?

Talkin Tarn

Selway, geology & landscape

Edenside, Carlisle

Events (not christenings)

Birth of children, family gatherings, and death of loved ones. Memorable sporting fixtures and triumphs, sun rises and sets. Snow scenes in 1947 and 1963. Seeing three types of kingfishers on the shore of Lake Awassa, Ethiopia.

Chance meetings – our best man – John Schofield who lives in British Columbia - in the Selkirk Arms in Kirkcudbright, Scotland, and Marianne our former Norwegian 'Au Pair' on a holiday in Havanna, Cuba.

Being at Wembley to see Pompey win the FA Cup in 2008

Small and unrecorded acts of kindness like a British lady, on a French camping site who, emerged from her caravan with a welcoming tray with tea and biscuits for a young German couple with a baby who had just arrived exhausted on the site next door.

Flying to Borneo on VSO in 1959 on a RAF cargo plane with atomic material on board, stopping off to refuel on a British base in the Sahara desert in Libya, (where pilgrims on the Haj were stuck) & the smell of Singapore before Lee Kuan Yu developed this city state.

Being made Lord Mayor of Portsmouth and welcoming 14 heads of State for the 50th Anniversary of D Day commemorative events in June 1994.

What events will you treasure on your death bed?

As Lord Mayor with WWII vet

Jazz festivals, especially Swanage

FA Cup Final, 2008

And clever church conversion (not cinemas into mosques)

Some religious buildings have become homes, warehouses, night clubs, and offices. Such building use changes to secular functions are to be found in our cities and towns, and even villages. Some are tasteful, others unusual and incongruous.

Just as civic associations give prizes to imaginative and appealing changes in the use and appearance of buildings, so too should the British Humanist Association Award give public recognition to eye catching conversions.

Here are some I have come across. Do you have some to share?

Solace and satisfaction

In the absence of an afterlife, at least we sceptics and humanists have people we love and admire – dead or alive; objects which we can treasure; places that mean a lot to us; events and achievements that make our life worth while. Our favourite music or books - *Raising the Human Spirit* compiled by Bryan Tully is full of inspiring prose and poems, Greg Epstein's Good *without God* is heartening and Marcus Brigstocke's *God Collar*, entertaining.

Finally, we can be heartened by signs of secularity we see around us – at least in Western Europe, if not in the rest of the World. Some of us are lucky to have been born into, live in, and will end our days in a relatively tolerant and secular society. Others are not lucky and need our help to survive and thrive in places where religion dominates and oppresses, especially at present in Bangladesh where humanists have been brutally killed.

We only have one life - let's make the best of it

CHAPTER 9
LET'S BE POSITIVE. What humanism can do for us and we can do for humanism

a) Leading a good life without religion

Here is what writers have to say about why and how, as humanists, we can and should lead socially useful lives.

Greg Epstein makes a plea for deeds not words. He asks…why be good? Why co-operate and help each other? His response is that giving and getting can be a win-win strategy. We will be better off when we co-operate. Direct reciprocity or indirect reciprocity . We do good to strangers – is it because we think God will punish us if do not? No, we humans…live our lives with the constant awareness that our behaviour can be seen and evaluated by others, for better or worse. Gossip and reputation can play a major role in influencing how we relate to others and treat them.

We also have evolved the ability to simply 'pay it forward'.

The parable of the father who lifts his young son onto his back to carry him across a flooded river is cited. 'When I am older', said the boy to his father, 'I will carry you across this river as you do now for me.' 'No you won't, said the father stoically. 'When you are older you will have your own concerns. All I expect of you is that one day you will carry your own son across this river as I now do for you…' 'Paying it forward can add a tremendous sense of meaning and dignity to our lives. Simply put, it feels good to give to others, whether we get it back or not.

He observes 'network reciprocity' - clusters of individuals bonding together and making an agreement to help one another without expecting direct return. Trusting each other and cooperating together.

Albert Camus in his intriguing book the *The Plague*, asks some fundamental questions – why we who do not believe in God, should be good. Compassion for humanity – a secular idiom to express the sentiment equivalent for – 'there but for the grace of God'

We can't change everything but, we can look around us and see how much we can change and how much we have changed.

Dignity is a goal to strive for. A direction to head in the willingness to assume responsibility for one's own life and to avoid surrendering that responsibility to any other person or institution.

Be aware of your own humanity and also other's humanity – all human beings are human.

Karen Armstrong's *The Character of Compassion* seeks input from people of every religious and ethical tradition – including humanism and atheism – may have 'a certain quality of Hallmark-card kitsch' to it, but few would argue with the sentiments and guidance expressed. Seek the best in yourself and others, pursue truth and honesty in all you do and be wary of allowing power, status or possessions to substitute for moral courage, dignity and goodness. Be positive and constructive, rather that negative and disrespectful.

In response to those around us who are sick, dying, or grieving for loved ones. Humanists seek to remember their lives and legacies. We try our best to carry on the good things. We learn from their mistakes. We do not paper over the deep wounds by saying – 'they are with God now'. We try to comfort one another, to offer hugs, kisses, time, patience, and presence, because no supernatural force can offer these things, and we need them.

The point of humanism is not just to collect little factoids, nuggets of knowledge about what we're supposed to do. The point is that we need to take concrete steps to put these ideas into practice in our daily lives.

Armstrong believes that naming ceremonies are noted as significant events. 'Choosing a name is an awesome responsibility, to carry with them for the rest of their lives two different cultural backgrounds, personal styles, family histories. It's a symbolic mutual project involving three people and it's wonderfully worth those people celebrating together.' Also choosing secular godparents to take a special interest in the child to guide parents' public commitment.

Follow the new Ten Commandments as set out by Richard Dawkins from an atheist website and augmented by some of his own.

- Do not do to others what you would not want them to do to you
- In all things, strive to cause no harm
- Treat your fellow human beings, your fellow living things, and the world in general with love, honesty, faithfulness and respect
- Do not overlook evil or shrink from administering justice, but always be ready to forgive wrong doing freely admitted and honestly regretted.
- Live life with a sense of joy and wonder
- Always seek to be learning something new
- Test all things, always check your ideas against the facts, and be ready to discard even a cherished belief if it does not conform to them
- Never seek to censor or cut yourself off from dissent: always respect the right of others to disagree with you
- Form independent opinions on the basis of your own reason and experience. Do not allow yourself to be led blindly by others
- Question everything

Added by RD are :

- Enjoy your own sex life (so long as it damages nobody else) and leave others to enjoy theirs in private whatever their inclinations.

- Do not discriminate on the basis of sex, race….(AND AGE! If you please)
- Do not indoctrinate your children
- Value the future on a time scale longer than your own

Below are some suggested axioms and actions for later life:

b) *Striving for a secular future, or at least an even playing field*

> **Papal overload**
>
> According to the census data there are about 5 million Roman Catholics in the UK. Likewise, there are at least 15 million who have no religion. Why then do we have so much coverage of the pope's resignation and so little about Jim Al-Khalili's recent choice as president of the British Humanist Association?
> **Dr Alan Burnett**
> *Southsea, Hampshire*

- Celebrate *special secular days/festivals* – eg Oct 1st (International Day of Older People), International Darwin Day on 12th February, and June21st (summer solstice) celebrated in America as World Humanist Day, In revolutionary France…' Fetes de la Vieillesse' were held in which local elders were praised, paraded and their homes decorated with garlands.

- *Be inspired by science* and 'mother nature', the evolutionary story and record, the beauty and diversity of flora and fauna around us, especially garden birds, familiar and nostalgic landscapes, and growing flowers and vegetables through the passing seasons

- *Write to newspapers* and contact the media with the humanist message.

- *Visit Conway Hall* in Red Lion Square in London, attend an event there and/or browse its excellent library.

- *Request secular books for your local library*. Some of the texts listed in chapter 10 are to be found in central libraries. However, they are grossly overwhelmed and outnumbered by religious volumes. It's time for a more balanced acquisition policy to be introduced.

- Draw quiet satisfaction from tasteful conversion of city centre and village churches into homes, art galleries and night clubs. Church closures we are told are due to a variety of causes including dwindling congregations – with 800 C of E parishes having 10 or fewer adults in regular attendance. Listed Churches and chapels make excellent community or senior centres where older folk can meet, eat, dance and sing. The UK is not alone in witnessing this secular change in the built environment. The Barnes study found that even in USA some 3,500 to 4000 churches closed every year. If you have the resources yourself, *buy a disused church and convert it to a secular use*, or more likely club together with others to do so. Organise a competition for the 'best conversion' of a former religious building.

- Reflect on a full and good life and pass on the message to the younger generation – achievements in jobs well done and how people of all ages – but particularly younger folk than ourselves, have benefited. Work with younger people on *intergenerational* humanist projects

- *Wear a T-shirt*, badge, tie or pendant with a secular message on it. American humanists have badges with the message – *I'm old, proud and a humanist. Why believe in a god, just be good for goodness sake, Born Again Atheist, This is probably the only life we've got – let's make the most of it, Reciprocity not ritual.* Look out for others who do not believe by observing those who refrain from kneeling or praying at funerals for example.

- Encourage and organise *humanist funerals* (without all the unctuous religious stuff from a clergyman who is a virtual stranger) with some good poems, readings and classical music followed by a lively wake when heart broken friends and family will remember the person who has died, celebrate his/her/my life and have a good time, preferable entertained by a jazz band.

- Join or form an *older people's forum* and/ or a *local humanist group* in your locality

- Look up the *local statistics for 'non belief'* in your city/town/district/neighbourhood from the Census and other sources and publicize the size and characteristics of the local 'non faith' community. Remind those in authority that this large majority, in some places, should be included in community and public life.

- Seeing and reminding others about *Christmas* and Easter and other 'religious' festivals are but palimpsests of earlier non Christian festivals.

- Campaign to remove the *religious bias* in national and local political and media institutions, polling, activities and pamphlets.

- Campaign for statues of Robert Ingersoll in every major American city, and Charles Darwin and Richard Dawkins in British ones. Blue plaques where eminent humanists lived.

- Distribute humanist literature where older people tend to be present - hospitals – waiting rooms, interfaith and no faith rooms, on wards; hospices and funeral establishments, including a list of local humanist celebrants and volunteers who can offer their services; community centres and surgeries; retirement homes and other specialist housing complexes for older people.

- A network of humanist intergenerational 'chaplains' not only to support university student/staff, but also older people living in university towns and cities. Establish an Institute of Humanist Studies at a major university with a retired university staff member.

- Aim for an even playing field, when it comes to humanists being invited to take part in public discussions in the media and in government. In addition to representatives of 'faith' groups, proponents of the secular view will, by law and common practice, be invited onto official bodies and panel discussions on radio or television. Those who have 'No religion' will be represented in direct ratio to their proportion of the population. That is, if in the 2031 census 50% of people do not claim to be affiliated or belong to, belief in or practice any religion then they should be given equal status as those who do, at every available opportunity.

- Get together with other like-minded older people and convert a disused pub, shop or church into a secular senior centre.
- Question the use of the spurious term 'faith communities'.
- Oppose the establishment of 'faith schools'.
- Organise a secular Sunday Assembly in your locality.
- Ask for books and pamphlets on humanism to be placed in local libraries, schools and community centres.
- Put this publication in a place where it can be found, picked up and read by older people. Send a copy to those who might like to read it.

c) *Let's be positively humanist*

Speculating about the future – forecasting what may and should happen is a bit of a rum business, as you are likely to some degree to be proved right or wrong at some time in the future. George Orwell's 1984 came and went. An essay in a book I edited in 1981 looked at possible geo-political developments – *Geopolitics in a shrinking world* by Stanley Brunn. – was an attempt to predict over thirty years ago – what the political map might look like in the twenty first century (Britain out of the EU. Who would have believed it?).

Let's think what sort of local community, city/county, region, country, continent and world we think might come into being in the first half of this century.

As a prominent American writer has said – 'The road ahead will not always be smooth, straight or pot-hole free'.
Richard Dawkins uses an imagined future as a 'raising consciousness' device, or as some would argue a polemical tool:

> Imagine, with John Lennon, a world with no religion. Imagine no suicide bombers, no 9/11, no 7/7, no crusades, no witch hunts, no gunpowder plot, no Indian Partition, no Israeli-Palestinian wars, no Serbs/Croat/Muslim massacres, no persecution of Jews as Christ-killers, no northern Ireland 'troubles', no honour killings, no shiny-suited, bouffant-haired televangelists fleecing gullible people of their money. Imagine no Taliban to blow up ancient statues, no beheadings of blasphemers, no flogging of female skin for the crime of showing an inch of it.

Not a bad start, although I fear injustices, conflicts and obscenities would remain, if, at some future (distant) date, a secular world did come into being.

But we will not be around to see what the world is like in the next century. Although there is a fair chance that our grandchildren will be. Maybe it's better to stick to the more immediate future – 2025, 2035, or even 2055.

The BBC are invited to broadcast a humanist event in Conway Hall, London; in Portsmouth, or elsewhere.

❦ Disbelief is widespread in the United Kingdom and growing. Likewise religious adherence and activity is gradually in retreat in most developed countries. Yet, although probably a majority of the adult population in Western Europe for example are 'disbelievers', and maybe 'atheistic' - they rarely call themselves 'humanists'. Many older people think and act in a secular way but do not see themselves as humanists and some of these will even have a religious funeral.

Can you blame older people in hospital from appreciating the good offices of a religious chaplain when there is no humanist one available? Or going along to the local church, mosque, temple or synagogue for a welcome bit of company? Or slipping a fiver into the collection box of the Salvation Army or Christian Aid?

The status quo will prevail until we humanists stand up and be counted, get a foothold in the public arena, and disseminate the message that a secular society can and does work and are 'good without God' in our lives.

Some readers of this publication will think that too much space is devoted to a light hearted critique of religion. This is indeed one of its purposes. But its main aim is to assist non religious older people in the UK, and elsewhere to be heartened by the words and examples of humanists.

Our numbers are growing, we are in good company, and future generations can build on our efforts.

CHAPTER 10
GOOD BOOKS AND RICH RESOURCES

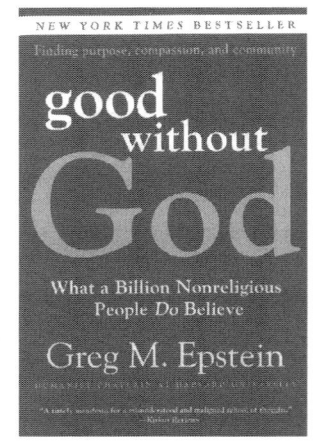

Allen South, Warren. *Who's Who in Hell. A Handbook and International Directory for Humanists, Freethinkers, Naturalists, Rationalists, and non Theists*, Barricade Books, 2000

Antony, Louise. *Philosophers without Gods. Meditations on Atheism and the Secular Life,* Oxford University Press, 2007

Armstrong, Karen. *Twelve Steps to Compassion,* Bodley Head, 2001

Armstrong, Karen. *The Case for God. What Religion really means.* Bodley Head, 2009

Berlingerblau, Jacques. *How to be Secular. A Call to Arms for Religious Freedom.* Mariner Books, 2013

Berman, David. *A History of Atheism in Britain. From Hobbes to Russell*, Croom Helm, 1988

Blackford, R and Schüklenk, U. (Eds) *50 Voices of Disbelief. Why we are Atheists.* Blackwell, 2009

Blackman, H.J. *Humanism,* Penguin, 1968

Brigstocke, Marcus. *God Collar,* Bantam Press, 2011

Browning, Guy. *Maps of my Life*, Vintage Books, 2009

Bruce, Steve. *Secularization,* Oxford University Press, 2011

Bulter-Sloss, Elizabeth. *Living with Difference. Report of the Commission on Religion and Belief in British Public Life.* Woolf Institute, 2015

Bupp, Nathan. *Meaning and Value in a Secular age. The Writings of Paul Kurtz.* Prometheus Press, 2012

Campbell, C. *Toward a Sociology of Irreligion,* Macmillan, 1971

Cave, Peter. *Humanism A Beginners Guide,* One World, 2009

Chopra, Deepak and Mlodinow, Leonard. *War of World Views Where Science and Spirituality Meet - And Do Not,* Three Rivers Press (CA), 2012

Coleman, Peter and Wilkinson, Peter. *Belief and Ageing: Spiritual Pathways in Later Life,* Policy Press, 2001. (Especially Chapter six – Coping without religious faith: Ageing among British Humanists.)

Copson, Andrew and Grayling, AC. (Eds) *The Wiley Blackwell Handbook of Humanism,* Wiley-Blackwell, 2015

Creeley, Roger. *The Best of Humanism,* Prometheus Books, 1988

Coyne, Jerry. *Why Evolution is True*, Oxford University Press, 2009

Cupitt, Don. *After God: the Future of Religion,* Weidenfeldt and Nicholson, 1997

de Botton, Alan. *Religion for Atheists* Hamish Hamilton, 2012

Dawkins, Richard. *The God Delusion.* Bantam Press, 2006

Dennett, Daniel. *Breaking the Spell. Religion as a natural phenomenon*, Penguin Books, 2006

Eagleman, David. *Sum: Tales from the Afterlives.* Canongate Books, 2009

Ehrenreich Barbara. *Living with a Wild God. A Non-believer's Search for the Truth About Everything.* Granta, 2014

Epstein, Greg. *Good without God.* William Morrow Harper Collins, 2009

Gould, Stephen Jay. *I Have Landed,* Jonathon Cape, 2002

Gaskin, JCA. (Ed*) Varieties of Unbelief from Epicurius to Sartre,* Macmillan, 1989

Grayling, A C. *The Good Book A Secular Bible,* Bloomsbury, 2011

Grayling, A C. *The Form of Things,* Orion Books, Weidenfeldt & Nicholson, 2009

Hancock, Jennifer. *Handy Humanism Handbook. 'A short and hopefully sweet introduction to the Philosophy of Humanism.'* (Available on line from the author)

Harris, Sam. *The End of Faith. Religion, Terrorism and the Future of Reason.* Norton, 2004

Harris, Sam. *The Moral Landscape,* Black Swan, 2010

Hitchens, Christopher. *The Portable Atheist,* Da Capio Press, 2007

Hitchens, Christopher. *God is not Great: How Religion Poisons Everything,* Atlantic Books, 2007

Holloway, Richard. *Looking in the Distance,* Canongate, 2004

Jacoby, Susan. *The Great Agnostic. Robert Ingersoll and American Freethought.* Yale University Press, 2013

Jewell, A. (Ed) *Ageing, spirituality and wellbeing,* Jessica Kingsley, 2004

Jones, Steve. *The Serpent's Promise The Bible Retold as Science,* Little Brown, 2013

Kennedy, Ludovic. *All in the Mind; A Farewell to God,* Hodder and Stoughton, 1999

Kitcher, Philip. *Living with Darwin.* Oxford University Press, 2007

Koenig, Harold et al. *Handbook of Religion and Health.* Oxford University Press, 2000

Konner, John. *The Atheist's Bible,* Duckworth Overlook. 2011

Lively, Penelope. *Ammonites and Leaping Fish: A Life in Time,* Penguin, 2014

Mackinley, Elizabeth. *The Spritual Dimension of Ageing,* Jessica Kingsley, 2001

Mason, Marilyn. *The Thinkers' Guide to Life.* Rationalist Press Association

Merchant, R. *Pioneering the Third Age. The Church in an Ageing Population,* Paternoster Press, 2003

Melly, George. *Slowing Down,* Viking/Penguin, 2005

Niblett, B. *Dare to Stand Alone. The Story of Charles Bradlaugh : Atheist and Republican.* Kramedart Press, 2010

OBrien, Joanne and Palmere, Martin. *The State of Religious Atlas.* Pluto/ Simon & Schuster, 1993

Ruse, Michael and Bullivant, Stephen. (Eds) *The Oxford Handbook of Atheism,* Oxford University Press 2013

Segal, Lynne. *Out of Time. The Pleasures and Perils of Ageing,* Verso, 2014

Sherine, Ariane. *The Atheist's Guide to Christmas,* Friday Books, 2009

Sloan Wilson, David. *Darwin's Cathedral; Evolution, Religion and the Nature of Society,* University of Chicago Press, 2002

Smoker, Barbara. *Free thought - Atheism – Secularization – Humanism,* GW Foote, 2002

Stoker, Barbara. *Humanism,* National Secular Society, 1984

Tully, Bryan. *Raising the Human Spirit.* Humanist Voice, 2016

Wolfe, Alan. *The Transformation of American Religion.* Free Press, 2003

Wright Willson, Jane. *Funerals Without God.* BHA

Zuckerman, Phil. *Living the Secular Life. New Answers to Old Questions*, Penguin Press, 2014

Assorted articles

Bruce, Steve. *The Pervasive World View. Religion in Post modern Britain British,* Journal of Sociology, 1997. Vol. 48

Grant, Bruce. *Fine Tuning the Peppered Moth Paradigm.* Evolution, 1999. Vol. 53

Longden, Gareth. *A profile of the British Humanist Association in Science,* Religion and Culture, *Vol 2*

Voas, David and Crockett, A. *Religion in Britain: neither Believing nor Belonging,* Sociology, 2005. Vol. 39

Voas, David and McAndrew, Siobhan. *Three Puzzles of Non-Religion in Britain,* Journal of Contemporary Religion, 2012. Vol. 27

See also the following - *Journal of Religious Gerontology, The Gerontologist, Ageing and Society, Journal for the Scientific Study of Religion.*

Additional resources, (see Epstein pages 227-239, especially for North America)

British Humanist Association

Evidence given by BHA to Age Concern's enquiry to Mental Health and Wellbeing in Later Life, 2006.

I Humanism, a chatty American humanist blog

Humanists for a Better World (info@h4bw.org.uk). A web-based interest group/network for UK humanists to share information and take collective action

List of friendly addresses to be found in Appendix of Richard Dawkins' *The God Delusion* for those needing support from escaping from religion, p.274 to 279

Lists of accredited BHA celebrants by locality in UK, for life cycle events – weddings, funerals, baby-naming.

Local humanist groups eg. South West London Humanists (first class website)

Online American Humanist Association bookstore – www.EvolveFish.com

The secular web – for Robert Ingersoll's works

Websites of local BHA groups and older people's forums

www.jen-hancock.com 6 reasons to be a humanist

www.robertingersoll.com to obtain images and reproductions of the great 19th century American humanist.

www.thehumanist.com, website of AHA

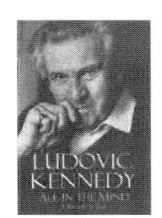

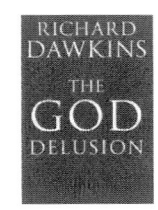

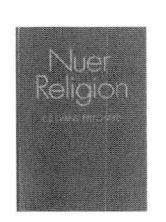

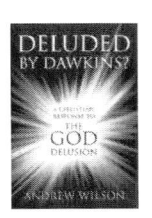

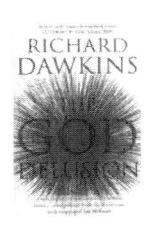

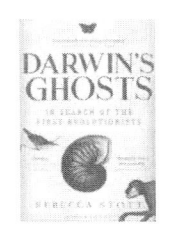

Are these books in your library?

PERMISSIONS

Every effort has been made to contact appropriate copyright holders to notify them of the intention to include quotes, short passages and illustrations, and seek their prior permissions.

A genuine attempt has been made to adhere to the UK Copyright Designs and Patients Act, 1988. If material has been included for which permission has not been granted, or mistakes have been made in the process of compiling this handbook, then the author takes full responsibility and will rectify, at the earliest opportunity, any omissions or errors brought to his attention.

The Illustrated Humanist Handbook for Older People is a family-funded, non-profit and locally published production. It is essentially a compilation and critical review of popular and academic contributions by a wide range of authors. Revisions will be made, where necessary, in any subsequent larger scale edition of this publication.

To achieve a 'fair deal' with authors and publishers whose work is quoted and embedded in the text, to the best of he author's knowledge, all quotes and short passages have been properly attributed. The names of many key authors are to be found in the acknowledgements section. In addition, the front covers of major texts are shown, together with a full bibliography. Most illustrations included are original - photographs taken by the author, specially commissioned cartoons and re-drawn maps.

Readers are invited to go to the books, journals and websites cited, and track down other original sources.

ADDITIONS

The author intends to have a second 'commercial' edition of this Handbook published in 2017. It will also be circulated electronically and via social media. Any errors and omissions will be rectified. Readers are invited to make constructive suggestions as to how this Handbook can be augmented and improved in content and format.

In particular additional illustrations are invited, for example, photographs of imaginatively converted churches, and cartoons. Personal testimonies and experiences of getting the humanist message over to older people are also solicited. Examples of secular funerals would also be welcome, as well as other publications and websites not mentioned in this edition. There is a wealth of material out there - it would be great to include some of it (fully acknowledged of course) in the next edition of the Handbook.

The author can be contacted by email: alanburnett@live.co.uk

TRICORN
BOOKS